MAULANA AZAD
A Pragmatic Statesman

(A Documentary Study 1923-42)

S.A.I. TIRMIZI

Commonwealth

MAULANA AZAD
A Pragmatic Statesman

(A Documentary Study 1923-42)

S.A.I. TIRMIZI

Commonwealth

MAULANA AZAD : A PRAGMATIC STATESMAN

Edition : 2026

ISBN 81-7169-104-8

Published by :

COMMONWEALTH PUBLISHERS (P) LTD.
4831/24, Govind Lane,
Ansari Road, Darya Ganj,
New Delhi - 110002
Ph. : 23272541, 23242541
e-mail : commonwealthpublishers2016@gmail.com

Distributed by :

ARJUN PUBLISHING HOUSE
4831/24, Govind Lane,
Ansari Road, Darya Ganj,
New Delhi - 110002
Ph. : 23272541, 23242541
e-mail : arjunbooks2001@gmail.com

Laser Typesetting by :

Dimple Computers
Delhi

Printed at :

Milan Enterprises
Delhi

Preface

In the birth centenary year of Maulana Abul Kalam Azad, a number of books have been written assessing various aspects of his multifaceted personality. Most of such books are in Urdu focussing mainly on his contribution to literature, journalism ond religious thought. These books largely ignore the crucial role he played in the national politics of his country. The English knowing scholars have usually been dissuaded from undertaking such a venture because of their lack of knowledge of Urdu in which language Maulana Azad mostly wrote.

Some scholars conversant with Urdu have no doubt made a serious attempt to pen down, in English, the biographies of Maulana Azad but these monographs too, like their counterparts in Urdu, focuss attention on his role as a religious thinker, litterateur and journalist and under value, if not totally ignore, the prominent part he played in shaping the course of India's struggle for freedom.

II

Assessing Maulana Azad's role in politics some scholars have concluded that he failed in his mission of Hindu-Muslim unity for which he worked so passionately throughout his life. Some scholars have alleged that Maulana Azad has judged the past from hindsight and is, therefore, quilty of Whig interpretation of history while some others even doubt his knowledge of English. It is true that the cause of Hindu-Muslim unity, so dear to Maulana Azad's heart, foundered on the rock of communalism but is it justified to ascribe this phenomenon to his personal failure? Did he not share this failure with other secular leaders of India's freedom movement? Was it not the failure of the Congress leadership which, ignoring his sober counsels, missed many opportunities of solving the communal tangle? Those who charge Maulana Azad with the Whig interpretation of history, do not seem to have taken notice of some of the hitherto unexplored private papers and other contemporary documents which go a long way in exposing the hollowness of such charges. The need for critical study of such documents cannot, therefore, be overestimated.

III

The present publication purports to fulfil this need to some extent. It contains 85 documents which, among others, include letters, telegrams statements, manifestos, appeals, press interviews, etc. Covering two crucial decades and spanning the period from Ist November, 1923 to 8th August, 1942 these documents have broadly been divided into two broad categories according to their form: (1) letters and telegrams and (2) statements and appeals. Within this formal categorisation they have been arranged chronologically.

I have adopted the chronological methodology because my approach in the treatment of the subject has been historical. This, I think, is absolutely essential for appreciating the significance of these documents in their historical context and the somewhat longish introduction is intended to provide the requisite historical perspective. As a corollary to this approach, I have endeavoured in the Commentary to furnish some useful information and have raised relevant points so very essential in understanding these documents which throw revealing light on the somewhat less illuminated political career of Maulana Azad as is evident from what follows.

IV

Three passions dominated the life of Maulana Abul Kalam Azad: love of learning, Hindu Muslim Unity and freedom of India. He was *priori* a scholar who strayed into politics. As an intellectual he shunned politics but was pushed into this area by the sheer force of circumstances. It was not he who sought politics but it was politics that sought him. Shy in nature and reserved in temperament, he, was too aloof to come close to the masses. He was too individualistic to accept the normal functions of a politician. The hectic political-life left him hardly any time for serious literary pursuits. He prized solitude which he got in prison where he got an opportunity to cultivate the life of the mind with the result that he wrote most of his monumental works—*Tazkira, Tarjumanul Quran* and *Ghubar i Khatir*-behind the British bars. While outside prison he preferred poring over books to political small talk. The conflicting spheres of scholarship and politics, therefore, impinged on each other and caused him mental tension. In the introduction to the *Tarjuman* he said, "the uproar of political activity and the calmness of literary life could not proceed together...I wish to bring the two together...I know the result. I have, therefore, no right to complain."

He succeeded, to some extent, in harnassing his scholarship to the cause of his second passion for Hindu-Muslim unity and developed his thesis of Fellowship of Faiths and the doctrine of Pluralistic Religious Co-existence. This paved the way for his political theory of Composite Nationalism which, rooted in the composite Indian culture, was secular in character. Imbibed as he was with the spirit of humanism, Maulana Azad considered Hindu Muslim unity more important than India's freedom. Presiding over the Special Congress Session at Delhi in 1923 he proclaimed, "The delay of *Sawaraj* will affect Indians but the end of our unity will be the loss to the entire human race."

Maulana Azad's approach to politics was entirely pragmatic. He exercised moderating influence on the Congress and zealously worked as a bridge-builder. He was responsible for bringing about reconciliation between the two rival groups of no-changers and pro-changers, the Gandhites and the *Swarajists*. Similarly when the abolition of the *Khilafat* disheartened the leadership in India, Maulana Azad took a pragmatic view of the whole matter and tried to channelise the anti-imperialist Muslim fervour into India's struggle for freedom. Similarly his approach to the Nehru Committee Report was pragmatic. The Report which did not contain any safeguards for Muslims was discussed by the All Parties Convention held on 28th December, 1928. The epitaph of the convention written by Maulana Azad ran: "The Muslims were fools to ask for safeguards and the Hindus were greater fools to refuse them". In the late twenties and thirties opportunities were missed for negotiating the communal question through constitutional means by conceeding some of the legitimate demands of the minorities. The Congress unfortunately took a rigid and unimaginative stand unheeding the magnanimous approach as suggested by Maulana Azad with the result that the cause of Hindu-Muslim unity, for which he worked so passionately, foundered on the rock of communalism.

Equally pragmatic was Maulana Azad's attitude to *ahimsa* or non-violence and war. He believed in non-violence only as a matter of policy and not as an article of faith as was the case with Mahatma Gandhi. When the World War II broke-out, Mahatma Gandhi did not want to "embarass" Great Britain and suggested unconditional support for the British on a non-violent basis. Jawaharlal Nehru thought that it was against the "dignity of India" to take advantage of her (England's) distress and rush at her throat. Maulana Azad's sympathies too lay with the Allies but he thought that India should participate in the war efforts only if its demands were fulfilled on 25th May, 1940 he wrote to Jawaharlal Nehru. "I do not know what is the *shan* (dignity) of India." We gave Britain fullest opportunity to take us with her but but she stubbornly refused to do so. We were forced to decide not to participate in this imperialistic War. We are not responsible for it. It lies with the imprudent vanity of the British Government. I do not understand how this confused and illogical conception could find a way to your mind." When the war took a serious turn for the Allies, Mahatma Gandhi declared, "We do not seek independence out of Britain's ruin" and Jawaharlal Nehru proclaimed, "England's difficulty is not India's opportunity." Maulana Azad thought that the immediate need was to demand a Provisional Government enjoying confidence of the people.

Maulana Azad tried to reconcile these conflicting views at the AICC meeting at Poona on 23rd-28th July, 1940 and observed in his opening remarks, "Honestly we cannot go as far as Mahatma Gandhi wants us to go. We admit that it is weakness on our part but it is a weakness which we share with the entire humanity." Thereafter the AICC passed the resolution to the effect that while the Congress must continue to adher strictly to the principle of non-violence in the struggle for independence, it was unable in the then prevailing circumstances to declare that the principle should be extended to free India's national defence." However, soon afterwards all but four members of the Congress Working Committee threatened to resign on the issue of India's participation in the War. As Congress President Maulana Azad was confronted with a situation similar to the one faced by Subhash Chandra Bose in the previous year. Should he revolt and organise another party like Bose? He had no large following in the Congress or outside. He had no option but to yield. The Congress Working Committee which met at Bombay on 13th-17th September, 1940 called upon all Congress organisations to stop all Civil Disobedience, individual or other, pending definite instructions from Mahatma Gandhi who regarded this suspension "as indispensible" for his forthcoming interview with the Viceroy." On 26th November, 1940 Maulana Azad reiterated at Lahore that "he was personally in favour of Mass Civil Disobedience but since they had entrusted everything to Mr Gandhi, they must carry out the Mahatma's programme. "A month later, in the course of an interview at Lahore on 30th December, 1940, he declared : "If India is invaded tomorrow and there is no other alternative to defend my country, I will not hesitate to take arms and fight." He was arrested and sentenced to 18 months imprisonment in Naini Jail.

V

The Japanese attack on Pearl Harbour on 6th December, 1940 forced the U.S.A. to enter into what became a global war. In order to test Congress reaction to the changed war situation, the British Government released Maulana Azad and Jawaharlal Nehru in the first week of December, 1941. When the Congress Working Committee met at Bardoli on 23rd to 30th December, 1941, Mahatma Gandhi, in his letter to Maulana Azad said, "On re-reading the Bombay resolution, I found that I had read into it a meaning which its letter did not bear...The discovery of the error makes it impossible for me to lead the Congress in the struggle for resistance to war effort on grounds in which non-violence was not indispensible. I could not, for instance, identify myself against Great Britain." Jawaharlal Nehru's sympathies, on the other hand, lay with the Allies "though he could not help in the war until the Congress demand for India's independence was conceded by Britain." Maulana Azad, however, maintained that "the issue before the Congress is not violence versus non-violence but in the British Government's attitude towards the Indian demand." The Congress Working Committee passed two resolutions. The first *inter alia* stated that "only a free India can be in a position to undertake the defence of the country" and the second resolution "relieved Mahatma Gandhi of his leadership of the Congress and suspended Individual Satyagraha in the face of successive Japanese air-raids.

When the successive Japanese lightening strikes in South-East Asia left the Allied forces reeling on every front, Generalissimo Chiang Kai-Shek arrived in Delhi and held talks with Maulana Azad and Jawaharlal Nehru on 11th February, 1942. In the course of the talks the Generalissimo observed that if the British Government offered self-government in the Dominion Status, the Congress should not reject it. Maulana Azad responded, "if during the war the British Government offered Dominion Status and agreed that Indian representatives could work with a sense of freedom and responsibility, the Congress would not refuse the offer." The Generalissimo, however, failed to convince the British Government.

Subsequently when the Viceroy announced to celebrate the China Day on 7th March, 1942 and Calcutta Radio approached Maulana Azad to record his message, he declined. When they informed him that Jawaharlal Nehru had already given them a message in this connection, he was terribly upset and on 23rd February, 1942 wrote to Jawaharlal Nehru, "our sympathy with China needs no further elucidation but would it be a proper way of expression to participate in the function fixed by the Viceroy for their own purpose?" In the meanwhile the fear of imminent Japanese attack made quite a few Congress leaders dizzy. Some of them even thought that the Japanese being Buddhists would cause no harm to Indians. Maulana Azad, however, thought otherwise. On 6th March, 1942 he wrote to C. Vijiaraghavachariar, "we do not want change of masters. Whether the new masters be more bad or less, we have no alternative but to refuse to submit and die with the satisfaction that we are dying like an honourable man."

VI

Pressurised by the India Office, the British Government sent Sir Stafford Cripps to resolve the political deadlock in India. Cripps arrived in Delhi on 23rd March, 1942 and released the Draft Declaration envisaging grant of Dominion Status to India. Some of the Congress leaders, including Sardar Vallabhbhai Patel, thought that the Allies were going to loose the War. Mahatma Gandhi had described the Cripps offer as "a post-dated cheque on a tottering bank". Maulana Azad and Jawaharlal Nehru thought otherwise and held discussions on behalf of the Congress but the negotiations failed on the issue of defence. On 10th April, 1942 Maulana Azad wrote to Cripps, "Popular resistance must have a national background and both the soldier and the civilian must feel that they are fighting for their country's freedom under national leadership".

Consequent upon rejection of the Cripps proposal the Congress Working Committee was divided on the line of action to be adopted for resisting the Japanese invasion. Sardar Patel, Rajendra Prasad and others supported Mahatma Gandhi's non-violent *Satyagraha* but Maulana Azad and Jawaharlal Nehru had serious reservations against launching a Civil Disobedience Movement at that juncture. They wished to co-operate with the Allies provided India was given real responsibility. Early in July Mahatma Gandhi told Maulana Azad that they could not work together and asked for his resignation but Sardar Patel intervened and the crisis was averted.

Mahatma Gandhi had been made to promise that the new movement would not be stopped merely for the reason that violence might be displayed. At the AICC on 8th August, 1942 Jawaharlal Nehru moved the Quit India Resolution and Maulana Azad fell in line. Speaking from the Chair, Maulana Azad made it abundanly clear that the Quit India demand did not mean physical removal of all Britishers from India but only meant transfer of power to Indian hands. Concluding his speech he observed that he was addressing a letter to President Roosevelt and approaching the Viceroy for an honourable settlement but the British Government took stern action by arresting the Members of the Congress Working Committee including Maulana Azad, Jawaharlal Nehru and Sardar Patel on 9th August, 1942 and despatched them to the Ahmadnagar fort

VII

Maulana Azad was, thus, a pragmatic statesman far ahead of his times. "Don't ask of Maulana's age" said Sarojini Naidu "he was fifty the day he was born." Sir Stafford Cripps viewed Maulana Azad as "the foundation and basis of India's future destiny." Lord Wavell was of the view that "with very few exceptions the Congress Working Committee are not an impressive lot; while there is a good deal of cleverness, there is no statesmanship among them (CWC). Azad came out well, he is honest, moderate and a gentleman but not a strong character...None (leaders) seems able to look beyond the immediate party anvantage. I believe, Azad is in many ways the best of them all."

Maulana Azad's contribution should, therefore, be assessed in the realm of ideas which constituted a vital motivating force for India's struggle for freedom. It is in this context that the study of Maulana Azad's ideas deserve serious consideration for the writing of the intellectual history of India's freedom movement.

In conclusion I must acknowledge the assistance I received from the officials of the Nehru Memorial Museum and Library and the National Archives of India. I am also grateful to Dr. (Mrs.) Najma Heptullah for encouraging me to undertake this task.

New Delhi
23rd November, 1990

S.A.I. TIRMIZI

Contents

PART II

STATEMENTS AND APPEALS

Introduction

Coming of a family of anti-imperialist Muslim divines who left India for Hijaz about the time of the Revolt of 1857[1], Muhyud Din Ahmad, with chronogramatic name of Firuz Bakht, was born in 1888 A.D. of a devout Arab mother and Sufi Indian father in Mecca where he studied the Quran and fundamentals of Arabic language which was his mother-tongue.[2] When he was hardly ten years old, the family moved to Calcutta where he finished his traditional Islamic curriculum at a comparatively young age under the strict supervision of his father. He was regarded as a reputed scholar when he was still in his teens and had started writing on religious and literary subjects in Urdu journals under the pseudonym of Abul Kalam Azad.[3]

His personality was moulded and his thoughts nurtured at Calcutta which was then not only the metropolis of British India but also a hub of intellectual activities which have had a great impact on the young mind. In Calcutta he read articles of Rashid Riza (1865-1935) and Shaikh Muhammad Abduh (d. 1905) in the Cairo Arabic periodicals *al-Hilal*, *al-Manar*

---

1. Maulana Abul Kalam Azad, *India Wins Freedom*, (Bombay, 1959), p. 1.
2. Abdur Razzaq Malihabadi *Azad ki Kahani Khud Azad ki Zabani* (Calcutta, 1959) pp. 181, 353.
3. Mushirul Haq, Art. Azad, Abul Kalam in *Dictionary of National Biography* (ed) S.P. Sen (Calcutta 1979), p. 93.

etc. He thus became acquainted not only with modern knowledge published in Arabic but also came to know of nationalist developments whether anti-British or anti-Ottoman.[1] This exposer to modern knowledge in Arabic revived his interest in the contemporary Arab world.

Thus exposed to a world wider than that of his father's house and gifted as he was with the faculty of original thinking and independent judgement, he naturally experienced a revulsion against the traditional form of education which laid emphasis on rote memory and tended to be imitative rather than innovative.[2] Averse as he was to treading the beaten path he got attracted to the writings of Shah Waliullah (1703-62) who had been an important figure in his intellectual background. He had discussed Shah Waliullah with his father who regarded himself as a disciple of his family. In his opposition to *taqlid* or imitation, Shah Waliullah had opened up the possibility of *ijtihad* or reinterpretation of Islam in the light of original sources especially the Quran and the Hadis. He struggled with the writings of Shah Waliullah in his youth and had only appreciated them later. He did, however, acknowledge Shah Waliullah as his intellectual forebear.[3]

While he was involved in this encounter with Shah Waliullah's doctrines, he got absorbed in the writings of Sir Sayyid (1817-98) who, like Shah Waliullah, was opposed to *taqlid* and favoured *ijtihad.* Maulana Azad was very much impressed by Sir Sayyid's socio-religious movement for extricating Muslim mind of obscurantism and intertia. He also supported Sir Sayyid's views on modern education and believed that a man could not be truely educated in the modern world unless he studied modern science, philosophy and literature. Sir Sayyid's writings stimulated his interest in the works of Al-Ghazali (d. 1111), *Ikhwanus* Safa and the

---

1. Ian Henderson Douglas, *Abul Kalam Azad : An Intellectual and Religious Biography*, (Delhi, 1988), p. 86.
2. *Ibid*; p. 41.
3. Malihabadi, *op. cit*; pp. 358-59.

Mutazilites which had not appropriately been emphasised in his traditional education.[1] The writings of Mutazilites reenforced his growing involvement in rationalism.

Sir Sayyid's influence spurred Maulana Azad's increasing interest in modern knowledge. He devoured almost all the Urdu translations of English books brought out by Sir Sayyid's Scientific Society. This introduced him to a wider world of science. It was again under Sir Sayyid's inspiration that he began to learn English under Muhammad Yusuf Jafari who taught him rudiments of the English language. He, then, read English Bible with the help of Urdu and Persian translations. This grounding in English enabled him to read English newspapers as also English books on history and philosphy.[2] This is borne out by his comments on English books in his personal library now housed in Azad Bhavan, New Delhi.[3]

While supporting the socio-religious movement of Sir Sayyid, Maulana Azad repudiated his mentor's pro-British politics. Sir Sayyid had enunciated the policy of loyalism to the British and prevented Muslims from participating in the political activities of the country. While Maulana Azad was getting disillusioned with Sir Sayyid's policies of loyalism and separatism, he met Maulana Shibli (1857-1914) for the first time at Bombay in 1904 though they had been in correspondence for some time past. They talked for half an hour and just before they parted, Maulana Shibli asked the young visitor if Abul Kalam was his father.[4]

Invited by Maulana Shibli, Maulana Azad joined *al-Nadwa* in 1905 and worked till March, 1906. He was responsible for introducing in this journal certain new features like Scientific News which is the evidence of his interest in Western learning aroused by Sir Sayyid. As Editor of

---

1. Douglas, *op. cit*; pp. 51-54.
2. Maulana Azad, *op. cit*; p. 3.
3. Sayyid Masihul Hassan, *Hawashi-i-Abul Kalam Azad* (Delhi, 1988) pp. 96, 188-95, 548, 569.
4. Douglas, *op. cit*. p. 72.

al-Nadwa, Maulana Azad had an opportunity to work with Maulana Shibli whose literaey companionship went a long way in blostering the youngman's self-esteem. Shibli's poetic imagination and style encouraged Maulana Azad to develop in similar direction.[1]

Pressed by Shaikh Ghulam Muhammad, proprietor of *Wakil*, Maulana Azad took over its editorship at Amritsar. It had the greatest influence and circulation of any Urdu newspaper and as such Maulana Azad thought that such a newspaper was the best instrument for publicising his thoughts but disturbed by the death of his brother and pressed by his father, Maulana Azad returned to Calcutta by the end of 1906.[2]

This was the time when Calcutta witnessed demonstrations against the Partition of Bengal and was in the throes of the Swadeshi Movement. Maulana Azad was impressed by the revolutionary activities of his compatriots and decided to join them in counteracting the British imperialist designs but he had hard time in gaining the confidence of his revolutionary associates. It was through the mediation of Shyam Sunder Chakraverty, an associate of Sri Aurobindo Ghose, that Maulana Azad was able to convince them that active hostility or even indifference of Muslims would make India's struggle for freedom much more difficult. He succeeded in finding a place in the secret parleys of Bengal revolutionaries.[3] Thus Maulana Azad made his debut into politics at the age of eighteen as later on claimed by him in his statement before the Presidency Magistrate in Calcutta (64).

Fired by the revolutionary fervour, Maulana Azad travelled through the Middle East in 1908 visiting Iraq, Egypt, Syria and Turkey where he met the followers of Sayyid Jamalud Din Afghani (d. 1897) who had sought to arouse the Muslim world against European imperialism. In order to counteract Western hegemony, Afghani advocated solidarity between Muslims and their non-Muslim compatriots in Egypt

---

1. Douglas *op. cit*; pp. 72-74.
2. Malihabadi, *op. cit.*, pp. 293-95.
3. Azad, *op. cit.*, p. 5.

and India. In Cairo Maulana Azad came into contact with some followers of Mustafa Kamil Pasha (1847-1908) who, under the influence of Afghani, regarded Britain as the unquestioned enemy and in 1907 had founded his *Hizbul Watan* or Nationalist Party which preached patriotism irrespective of religion and language and maintained that true religion preaches true patriotism and as such there should not be any conflict between the spheres of religion and national life.[1] When he went to Turkey, he established contacts with some of the leaders of the Young Turk Movement. Maulana Azad had to cut short his travels because of his father's illness and had to return to Calcutta.[2]

Contacts with Muslim revolutionaries abroad convinced Maulana Azad that their fervour was of the same order as that of the Hindu revolutionaries of Bengal. Their common consuming passion was liquidation of British imperialism. This confirmed Maulana Azad's political beliefs and he felt that God had called him to arouse Muslims of India and to persuade them to join the movement for political liberation.

Crystallization of his political ideas, more or less, synchronized with the formulation of his religious thoughts. Though tutored in traditional sciences, the extracurricular reading, particularly the writings of Sir Sayyid, led Maulana Azad to a mental crisis. He observed, "there is no positive conviction of my heart which was not pricked by all the thorns of doubt and there is no belief of my soul which has not passed through all the tests of unbelief and denial." In fact he passed through the stages of dogmatism, then scepticim followed by denial and repudiation and then a real rapproachment. Ultimately he discovered that the fundamentals of all religions are same. It is the adultration which is the cause of differences. These differences would automatically disappear if all the religions were restored to their pristine state.[3]

---

1. Douglas, *op. cit.*, pp. 84-85.
2. Maulana Azad, *op. cit*; pp. 6-7.
3. Douglas, *op. cit*; p. 94.

In order to propagate his ideas and to build up public opinion, Maulana Azad launched his Urdu weekly *al-Hilal* in 1912. It had two main objectives. Firstly to revive in Muslims the true spirit of Islam and to reorganise their religious and social life. Secondly to infuse in them the spirit of freedom as enjoined upon them by Islam. In the domain of religion *al-Hilal* challenged traditional *taqlid* and offered fresh interpretation of Islam as related to contemporary life. Its influence was prodigious, especially among the elite. The paper shocked the conservatives and created furore in political circles. It criticised the 'loyal' attitude of the Aligarh Movement to the British and the "hostile attitude of the British to the Muslim world in general."[1]

When *al-Hilal* was launched the Tripolitan and Balkan war against the Turks had roused sympathies for those who suffered at the hands of imperialism[2] and alineated Muslim opinion in India against the British. This resulted in giving rise to the tide of Pan-Islamic feeling among the Indian Muslims. Maulana Azad used *al-Hilal* to undermine confidence in the loyalism that he saw at Aligarh. His primary purpose was to whip up enthusiasm in Indian Muslims for opposing the alien rule. Maulana Azad's Pan-Islamism, was not something that gave way later to Indian nationalism. From the very beginning it served the interests of his nationalism.[3] A thorough investigation of the files of *al-Hilal* leaves no doubt that Maulana Azad from the very outset saw the necessity of Muslims and Hindus working together to oppose the British imperialism.

When there were no longer wars against Muslims in Europe, Maulana Azad began to direct attention of his readers to South Africa. He felt that Muslims must concern themselves not only with Tripoli and the Balkans but also with South Africans. This was in consonance with the nationalist feeling in India. He observed, "if the whole world is our country and

1. Mushirul Haq *op. cit*; p. 93.
2. Douglas, *op. cit*; p. 25.
3. *Ibid*; p. 149.

to be honoured, the dust of India has the first place......If all mankind are our brothers, then Indians had the first place but Muslims should be aroused more than anyone by the troubles in South Africa . . . because they came to save the whole world."'[1] He also drew the attention of his readers to Mahatma Gandhi who was suffering imprisonment for his activity on behalf of the Indian community in South Africa. On 26 November, 1913 he wrote that it was because of him (Mahatma Gandhi) that 'the fire burns in the hearts of all Indians in South Africa.[2] The next week's issue of *al-Hilal* carried a picture of Mahatma Gandhi on the front page.

Maulana Azad wanted that the Muslim agitation for freedom should not be isolated from that of other Indians but must be in conjunction with them. In December, 1913 the Congress meeting in Karachi provided him an opportunity to criticise Muslims for their past aloofness and to praise the policies of the Congress. He observed that the policy of separatism of the Muslim League was outdated and maintained that even those Muslims who do not want to admit it in public would acknowledge privately that the Congress was the one party that had consistently and honestly championed Indians' rights.[3]

Maulana Azad's messianic zeal led him to consider *al-Hilal* as only a part of the larger movement which he intended to lead. Inspired by the *Hizbul Umma* or Peoples Party and *Hizbul Watan* or Nationalist Party founded in 1907 by the followers of Muhammad Abduh and Mustafa Kamil respectively,[4] Maulana Azad organised in 1913 his *Hizbullah* or Party of God which would unite all Indians in liberating India which was the bastion of British imperialism.[5]

When World War I brokeout in 1914 the Bengal Government was disturbed by the anti-imperialist policy of *al-Hilal*

---

1. *Al-Hilal* 3 (22); 395-98.
2. *Ibid*; 3 (22) : 397; 23 : 412.
3. Douglas, *op. cit*; p. 145.
4. *Ibid*; p. 115.
5. *Ibid*; p. 97.

which was banned in 1914. From 12 November 1915 Maulana Azad started a new weekly *al-Balagh*, from Calcutta which was also banned.[1] The activities of Maulana Azad now came to be closely watched by the C.I.D. which soon discovered that he was the moving spirit behind the Silk Letters Conspiracy and had worked out a plan in collaboration with Shaikhul Hind Maulana Mahmudul Hasan and Maulana Obedullah Sindhi to liberate India with the help of trans-frontier revolutionaries to whom he was reported to have sent Bengali bomb-makers and doctors. Maulana Obedullah Sindhi succeeded in joining the first Provisional Government of India in Kabul with Raja Mahendra Pratap as President and Barkatullah as Prime Minister. Maulana Azad used to keep contact with Raja Mahendra Pratap when he was organising his revolutionary movement in Kabul. He could not go to Kabul as he was interned on 20 May, 1916 at Ranchi under the Defence of India Act.[2]

It was during this long forced withdrawal from active political life that Maulana Azad wrote his *Tazkira* which was intended to be an autobiography but branched off into the story of heros of Islam and his anti-establishment ancestors. His ideal in the *Tazkira* was Ibn Taimiya (1268-1328), who not only opened the gates of *ijtihad* but also opposed the *uluma* of his time who were subservient to the Mongol rulers in order to safeguard their own position. Maulana Azad felt that Ibn Taimiya's stand was similar to the resistance he himself felt compelled to offer to the Pro-British attitude of the leaders of the Aligarh School of thought.[3] Besides the *Tazkira* he commenced writing his Commentary on the Quran wherein he propounded the theory of Fellowship of Faiths and propagated the doctrine of Pluralistic Religious Co-existence. He was thus feeling his way towards his political theory of Composite Nationalism for which he found sanction in the

---

1. Mushirul Haq, *op. cit.*, pp. 93-94.
2. NAI, Home Political. A. June, 1919, No. 590, Appendix. I.
3. Douglas, *op. cit*; p. 169.

Quran and a precedent in the Covenant of Madina.[1]

When the World War I ended, Maulana Azad was released after three and a half years of internment on the last day of 1919. During his internment at Ranchi, the Jalianwala Bagh massacre had set the whole country afire. The Indian Muslims were particularly wild with rage on account of the behaviour of the British and her allies with Turkey whose Ottomon Sultan was also their Khalifa. In order to preserve the Khilafat, a movement was launhed at Delhi on 23 November 1919 by Ali Brothers and was subsequently supported by Mahatma Gandhi.

The Khilafat Movement was in full swing when Maulana Azad came out of internment. On 18 January, 1920 Hindus and Muslims had assembled in Delhi in order to wait in deputation upon the Viceroy and place before the Government the sentiments of the Indian Muslims with regard to Turks. Maulana Azad who met Mahatma Gandhi for the first time at this meeting put his signature to the memorial to be submitted to the Viceroy but did not join the deputation because he felt that "these methods-begging, petitioning, waiting in deputation and so on—could not be of much avail. We have to try to find some means of exerting direct pressure."[2] Presiding over the Khilafat Committee meeting in Calcutta in February, 1920 Maulana Azad gave a most comprehensive exposition of the Khilafat Movement's religio-political programme. It was at this meeting that he presented the programme of non-co-operation.[3] Aware as he was of the writings of the Arab nationalist opponents of the Ottomans, Maulana Azad threw his weight behind Khilafat Movement because he found that nationalism and Khilafatism were organically related as the avowed twin objects of the entire country.[4] The All India Khilafat Committee adopted Non-Co-operation as its programe four months before the Congress did so. In the formulation of

---

1. Douglas, *op. cit*; pp. 210, 289.
2. Moin Shakir, *Azad, Islam and Nationalism* (New Delhi) pp. 22-23).
3. Malik Ram (ed),*Khutbat-i-Azad*, (Delhi, 1974) pp. 47-55.
4. Douglas, *op. cit*; p. 177.

Non-Co-operation programme Maulana Azad was no less responsible than Mahatma Gandhi[1], though the latter subsequently became the sole exponent and practitioner of the idea.

This approach of Maulana Azad brought him very close to Mahatma Gandhi with the result that when the latter presented the programme of Non-Co-operation to the Khilafat leaders, they asked for some time to ponder over the programme but Maulana Azad accepted it without a moment's hesitation.[2] Maulana Azad's prime object in supporting Non-Co-operation programme was to whip up enthusiasm in the Indian Muslims for opposing their non-Muslim British rulers. In order to propagate the idea of Non-Co-operation among the people the Congress leaders, including Mahatma Gandhi, Ali Brothers and Maulana Azad toured the country. The All India Khilafat Conference held at Karachi on 8 July, 1921 passed a resolution that "it is unlawful for any faithful Muslim to serve from that date in the army or help or acquiesce in their recruitment.[3] The British Government retaliated by arresting leaders throughout the country. Maulana Azad was charged with instigating revolt by his two speeches which he delivered at Mirzapur in July, 1921. In these speeches he was reported to have urged Indians in general and Muslims in particular to start a campaign of Non-Co-operation. He was arrested on 10 December, 1921.[4] He had to face a fairly long trial. The Chief Presidency Magistrate in his judgement delivered on 9th February, 1922 observed, "The Maulana had through his speeches tried to spread a feeling of ill-will and hatred against the established laws of the Government and therefore found himself guilty."[5]

For his appearance before the Chief Presidency Magistrate Maulana Azad wrote out a statement that goes a long way to

---

1. Hiren Mukerji, *Recalling India's Sttruggle for Freedom*, Delhi, 1983, p. 94.
2. Maulana Azad, *op. cit*; pp.10-11.
3. Pattabhi Sitharamayya, *The History of the Congress* (Allahabad, 1935), p. 365.
4. Douglas, *op cit*; p. 180.
5. A.B. Rajput, *Maulana Abul Kalam Azad*, (Lahore, 1946), p. 99.

show how very conscious he was of the part he was playing in the drama of history. He saw himself cast in the same role as that of Jesus, Socrates, Gallileo, all victims of unjust courts. In fact from 1910 until his imprisonment in 1921 he thought himself as sort of *Mujaddid* (Religious Reformer) or at the head of *Hizbullah* which would unite all Indians in liquidating the British Imperialism.[1] Later on referring to this trial Maulana Azad wrote, "The trial was agonizing and yet I tried to rise equal to the occasion-This was a bitteres. cup fate ever held to my lips. I drank its contents without the slighest demur". Maulana Azad was awarded one year's rigorous imprisonment on 9th February, 1922.[2]

Two days after Maulana Azad's imprisonment, Mahatma Gandhi abruptly called off Non-Co-operation Movement following the news of the burning of 22 policemen by angry peasants at Chauri Chaura in Gorakhpur District. This resulted, in a sense in anti-climax and disillusionment. Frightened by unprecedented support Muslims gave to the Non-Co-operation Movement, the British imperialists started to fan hostilities between Hindus and Muslims through communal organisations. The Hindu Mahasabha joined hands with the Arya Samaj in its campaign of *Shuddhi* or Purification and *Sanghatan* or Organisation which provoked *Tabligh* or Propagation and *Tanzim* or Organisation among Muslims. The unparalleled Hindu-Muslim unity of 1919-1922 was quickly followed by communal riots on an unprecedented scale.

When Maulana Azad was released from Alipore jail on 1st Janaury, 1923 he found that the political climate in the country had completely changed. The Hindu-Muslim unity so dear to his heart had eroded. In order to restore communal harmony, he, along with C.R. Das, Motilal Nehru. Hakim Ajmal Khan and Sarojini Naidu, toured the affected areas. They visited Punjab in the latter half of March 1923 and the

1. Douglas, *op, cit*; p. 9.
2. Humayun Kabir, *Maulana Azad : A Memorial Volume*, (Bombay 1959), p. 128.

first week of April, 1923. They issued a statement on 4th May, 1923 on the intercommunal situation in the Punjab (65).

Equally perturbed was Maulana Azad on the split that had taken place at the Gaya session of the Congress presided over by C.R. Das. The No-Changers wanted to continue Mahatma Gandhi's policy of non-violent Non-Co-operation but the Pro-Changers wanted to contest elections to the new reformed Councils. Thus, there was a rift among the Congress leaders over the Council Entry Programme. The Pro-Changers including C.R. Das and Motilal Nehru formed the Swaraj Party.[1] In order to bring about ammicable settlement between the apposing groups, C.R. Das offered to resign from the Congress Presidentship at the meeting of the All India Congress Committee held on the day Maulana Azad came out of jail. The compromise formula evolved by Maulana Azad was unanimously accepted by the Congress Working Committee which met at Bombay on 1st February, 1923. It was Maulana Azad's moderating influence, according to Acharya J B. Kripalani, that avoided a cleavage at the time between the Pro-Changers and the No-Changers. Subsequently Maulana Azad was elected president of the Special Session of the Congress which met at Delhi on 15th September, 1923. At the age of thirty five he was the youngest man ever to preside over the Congress. The prime purpose of this Special Session was to heal the factional rift between the Pro-Changers and the No-Changers. In his presidential speech he said, "Unity is all that we need and it is in order to establish it that we have gathered here to day". He called non-violence the soul of Non-Co-operation and asserted, "if non-violence be not accepted as an article of faith, it is enough if it be accepted expedient and politic". In this address he explicitly dealt with Hindu-Muslim unity and observed, "India being inhabited by people of different religious persuasions, prejudices, disturbances, now and then, were quite possible but the remedy lay in not giving them a sectarian colour but to blame

1. Maulana Azad, *op. cit*; p. 12.

the guilty and sympathise with the wronged party". Later in the speech he observed, "If today an angel descending from the clouds were to declare from the top of the Qutab Minar in Delhi, discard Hindu-Muslim unity and within twenty-four hours Swaraj is yours, I would prefer to sacrifice Swaraj rather than Hindu-Muslim unity, for delay in the attainment of Swaraj will be a loss to India alone, but if our unity disappears, it will be a loss to the whole world of humanity". He concluded his address with these words, "I appeal to both communities not to trample so cruely upon the national aspirations and hopes—our determination, our courage, our patriotism are under a very great trial". This remarkable address reflects the human values so dear to Maulana Azad's heart. Such ideas were not new to him. They had come to him as a solution to his youthful confusion concerning multiplicity of religions and had led him to evolve the theory of pluralistic religious co-existene. The Special Delhi Session of the Congress considerably suceeded in terminating the domestic squabbles of the Congress and in arresting the rapid spread of inter communal bitterness. Urging the people of all communities to show tolerance and regard for each other's religious ideas a Manifesto was issued on 8th October 1923 over the signatures of Maulana Azad, Motilal Nehru. C. Rajagopalachari and Hakim Ajmal Khan. In order to grapple with the recrudence of the communal differences as also to revitalise the Congress Committees to meet the challenge of the formidable communal evil, Maulana Azad thought it imperative to resume the adjourned deliberations of the session of the Congress. In consultation with Hakim Ajmal Khan, Pandit Madan Mohan Malaviya, Lala Lajpat Rai, Motilal Nehru, Sarojini Naidu, Dr. M.A. Ansari and some other friends, Maulana Azad called at Delhi on 30th November, 1923 an informal conference of leading Congressmen for devoting their earnest thoughts to the questions of the hour with a view to evolve a mature and effectual programme of work to be placed before the Cocanada Congress. He, therefore, issued on 1st November, 1923 a circular letter inviting the leading Congress men to the Conference (I).

In the meanwhile the Khilafat Movement continued as a pale reflection of its former self till the Turks exiled Abdul Majid and abolished the Khilafat in March 1924. This proved devastating to the Khilafatists like Maulana Muhammad Ali but Maulana Azad was not disturbed and tried to redirect the energies of the Indian Khilafat Committee into work for education, social reform, and economic advancement of Indian Muslims. His enthusiasm for the Indian freedom movement was unimpared and he felt that the matters closer at home now deserved greater attention.[1]

The matter that attracted Maulana Azad's immediate attention was the communal riots which broke out at Nagpur early in 1924 on the issue of playing of professional music in front of mosques. In order to restore communal harmony Unity Conference was held at Delhi on 26th September, 1924 under the presidentship of Motilal Nehru. Maulana Azad actively participated in this conference which passed resolution declaring that "all the points in dispute shall be decided by reference either to private arbitration or, where that is impossible, by reference to a Court of Law."[2]

In order to arbitrate in the Hindu-Muslim dispute Maulana Azad and Motilal Nehru visited Nagpur on 11th, January, 1925 and on the following day held a meeting with a view to go in to the question. The arbitrators had most pleasant surprise in store for them. At the commencement of the proceedings it was stated on behalf of Muslims that "while they fully believed that there was a custom to stop all music when passing their Mosques, they had after full consideration of the matter and in the interests of an abiding unity between the two communities determined to surrender their legal right and to leave it to the good sense of the Hindus to play or stop music as they thought fit" (66). Subsequently Dr. Moonje,

1. Ghulam Rasul Mihr, *Tabarrukat i Azad* (Hyderabad, 1959), pp. 214-60.
2. Subramania Iyer, *Role of Maulana Abul Kalam Azad in Indian Politics* (Hyderabad, 1968), p.37.

as president of the public meeting addressed by the arbitrators, assured the Muslims on behalf of the Hindus of Nagpur that "the brotherly feelings of the former (Muslims) would be fully reciprocated by the latter (Hindus)". Maulana Azad and Motilal Nehru in their press statement of 13th January, 1925 thanked both the parties at the happy settlement arrived at (66).

Besides Nagpur the other places affected by the communal frenzy were Calcutta, Delhi and Allahabad. In fact the entire country was ablaze with the communal fire of the Kohat riots since September, 1924.[1] Maulana Azad and Motilal Nehru wanted to put an end to the long drawn out riots and with this end in view they issued on 31st July, 1926, a Manifesto wherein they explicitly pointed out, "our present troubles are due to the fact that by an indiscriminate mixing up of the political and religious issues, we have initiated a rerivalist section which because of the existence of heterogeneous elements in our country, makes a cultural and social conflict inevitable and it is clear that the only real remedy which can save us from disaster, is the deliberate establishment in our midst of a national conciousness and a national atmosphere in which religious and communal conflicts and passions will be relegated to a subordinate and a lower plane" (67).

In order to combat communalism the Manifesto maintained, "we have decided to start a movement to rally to a centre and organise those sections of enlightened Indians who agree with us that communalism is a negation of nationalism" (67). In order to achieve this objective the Manifesto prescribed the following three guiding principles: (1) full liberty of religious views and practices; (2) absolute tolerance of the views and practices of others; (3) adjustment of communal relations on the basis of strict legal rights of communities and individuals (70). In order to avoid communal conflicts and to bring about a thorough understanding between the different communities on a solid and permanent basis the Manifesto

---

1. Iyer *op. cit.*, p. 41.

proposed establishment of the Indian National Union. A preliminary meeting of those who expressed their willingness to join the proposed Union was held at Delhi on 10th September 1926. A sub-committee consisting of Maulana Azad, Sarojini Naidu, K. Santhanam and others was appointed to draft the rules and regulations of the Union.[1]

Hindu-Muslims unity was in the air but Hindu-Muslim riots were on the *terra firma* in 1927. The worst affected places were Lahore, Nagpur, Bihar, Bareily and Multan. S. Srinivasa Iyengar wanted to evolve a formula for Hindu-Muslim unity. On 25th June, 1927, Maulana Azad suggested Calcutta as the venue for the Unity Conference (2). The All India Congress Committee ultimately organised Unity Conference on 27th October, 1927 which was chaired by S. Srinivasa Iyengar.[2]

In the following year when Simon Commission came to India it was greeted with black flags and shouts of "Simon go back" because no Indian was included in this Indian statutory commission. A joint statement, signed by Maulana Azad, Dr. M.A. Ansari, Maulana Muhammad Ali, Lala Lajpat Rai, M.A. Jinnah and others, was published in which they reiterated their decision that they "cannot have any thing to do with the Commission at any stage or in any form.[3] The Congress now took the initiative and called an All Parties Conference under the presidency of Motilal Nehru to draft a constitution acceptable to Indians. The Nehru Committee Report did not contain any safeguard for Muslims as demanded by Muslim League. This Report was discussed by the All Parties Convention held at Calcutta on 28th December, 1928. The epitaph of the Convention was written by Maulana Azad which ran as follows : "The Muslims were fools to ask for safeguards and the Hindus were greater fools to refuse

---

1. Iyer, *op. cit.*, pp. 42-43.
2. *Ibid.*, pp. 43-44.
3. *The Indian Quarterly Register*, I 1928, p. 65.

them".[1] Jinnah was against the acceptance of the Nehru Report.

Maulana Azad in his telegram of 4th May, 1929 asked Motilal Nehru to add his name to the signatories to the Manifesto advising Muslims to co-operate with Congress on the Nehru Report (3). Those who accepted the Nehru Report broke away from the Muslim League and formed a new party called the All India Muslim Nationalist Party under the presidency of Maulana Azad with T.A. Sherwani and Dr. M.A. Ansari as Secretary and Treasurer respectively. The aims and objects of the new party which worked within the Congress were as follows : (1) to counteract the reactionary activities of the so called All India Muslims Conference ; (2) to promote a spirit of nationalism among Muslims ; (3) to develop a mentality opposed to communalism and (4) to induce Muslims and Hindus to treat the other in a spirit of broad minded patriotism.[2]

The Congress Working Committee met at Lahore under the presidentship of Jawaharlal Nehru on 2nd January, 1930 and resolved to implement the Congress resolution of Purna Swaraj or complete independence and to observe 26th January, as the Purna Swaraj Day all over India. As authorised by the Muslim Nationalist Party, Maulana Azad and Dr. M.A. Ansari issued on 2nd January, 1930 an appeal saying, "we have no doubt in our minds that Musslamans owe it to their motherland to respond to the historic call of the Congress and join it with cheerful determination to see the national struggle through"(68).

In order to achieve Purna Swaraj Mahatma Gandhi launched non violent Civil Disobedience Movement popularly called Salt Satyagraha on 14th February, 1930. There was widespread picketing, demonstrations and hartals all over the country followed by arrests of Congress leaders. Maulana Azad was arrested on 21st August, 1930 and was imprisoned for six months in the Meerut District Jail where he could

1. K.M. Munshi, *Pilgramage to Freedom* (Bombay), 1947, p 25.
2. Iyer, *op. cit.*, p. 57.

find time to finish two volumes of his monumental *Tajumanul Quran.* The distinguishing feature of his commentary of *suratul fatiha* is the thesis of *Wahdat-i-din* (Fellowship of Faith) He propounded the thesis that mankind was at first one people but later split up. Although this basic *din* (faith) was always the same, there were differences in the *shara* (law) which were necessitated by varying social conditions. The deviations from the basic *din* have resulted in religious sectarianism. It was to rectify these deviations that God sent prophets in every place and in every age but their message was the same.

In the meanwhile in consequence of the statement made by the British Prime Minister on 19th January, 1931 Lord Irwin, Viceroy of India, released the Congress leaders including Mahatma Gandhi and Maulana Azad. As a result of long negotiations Gandhi-Irwin Pact was signed on 5th March, 1931. The British Government agreed to put an end to all repressive measures and Mahatma Gandhi publically halted the Civil Disobedience Movement. The radical Congress leaders read in this Pact nothing but capitulation to the Government. The frustration and anger of radical Congressmen was sharppened by the execution of Bhagat Singh, Sukhdev and Raj Guru on 23rd March, 1931 just two days before the opening of the Karachi Congress on 26th March, 1931 which approved Mahatma Gandhi's stand.

While the Karachi session of the Congress was going on, serious communal riots broke out in a number of cities including Mirzapore, Benares, Agra and Kanpur. The tragedy at Kanpur resulted in a large number of deaths including that of Ganesh Shankar Vidyarthi who died while rescuing those in danger (69). Maulana Azad and other Congress leaders issued an appeal and said, "we are convinced that there are more points of contact and common interest between us, the infinitely less of differences. Chief among the former is the economic life which is impossible to be led in isolation. Common birth makes us interdependent in daily life. It is easy enough to see that both must perish if each lived its daily life apart from the other. He, therefore, who parts the two and sets one community against the other, is the enemy of his own and must be treated as such. At this juncture we cannot lay too much stress upon the necessity of not magnifying every petty quarrel into a communal grievance and using it as a signal for strife" (69).

The Communal Award announced in mid-August, 1932 by Ramsay Mac Donald expanded the separate Muslim electorate formula to include Sikhs, Indian Christians, Anglo-Indians and depressed classes. The Award was greatly resented by the Hindus. Mahatma Gandhi entered into Poona Pact with Dr. B R. Ambedkar and succeeded in retaining modifications so far as the depressed class representation was concerned but the more important question of the Muslim representation remained unsolved. Maulana Azad tried to persuade the Muslim leaders to arrive at a settlement on the basis of the acceptance of thirteen out of fourteen points of Jinnah and joint electorate in accordance with the formula of Maulana Muhammad Ali.

In order to explore the avenues of honourable and permanent settlement Unity Conference was held at Allahabad on 23rd November, 16th December and 23rd December 1932 under the presidentship of Vijiaraghavachariar. Eminet leaders like Madan Mohan Malviya, C. Rajagopalachari, Maulana Shaukat Ali, Rajendra Prasad participated in the deliberations. The participants were immensely influenced by the prevailing cordiality. The Unity Conference came very close to a solution of the communal problem but difference of opinion on one or two small matters prevented a settlement. The British Government was not slow to see the danger to itself from the earnest efforts afoot for the solution of the communal problem.

In the meanwhile Mahatma Gandhi continued to pursue his anti-untouchability campaign which was opposed by the orthodox Hindus. Perplexed by these developments, he went on twenty one day self-purification fast on 8th May, 1933 in the Yeravda jail. The British Government immediately set him free. Mahatma Gandhi temporarily suspended the Mass Satyagraha and recommended individual civil resistance instead. He asked the Government to release the civil resistors. Willington, the Viceroy, declined to accept the suggestion unless the movement was unconditionally abandoned. Subhas Bose and other radical leaders of the Congress were outraged. They maintained that the Mahatma Gandhi as a political leader had failed and insisted that "the Congress required fresh leadership and radical reorganization".[1] One section of Congressmen held that either there should be mass resistance or no resistance at all. Another section was of the opinion that it was necessary to revive the Swaraj Party in order to contest the coming elections and enter the Councils. Maulana Azad held the view that "it was not only the right but it was the duty of every Congressman who for some reason or other did not want to or could not take part in civil resistance and who had faith in entry into the legislatures to seek entry and form combinations in order to prosecute the programme.[2]

As regards Council Entry it was decided to contest elections for which a Parliamentary Board was appointed. Maulana Azad was first a member of the Board and then become its president when Madan Mohan Malviya resigned on 26th July, 1934. Subsequently when the British Government lifted the ban, the All India Congress Committee met on 26th October, 1934 at Bombay under the presidentship of Rajendra Prasad. It was at this session that Mahatma Gandhi announced, "I see that the educated and intelligent sections of the Congressmen no longer have faith in my programme of work......I think, therefore, it would be appropriate and in the interest of the Congress that I should withdraw myself from Congress" but Maulana Azad and others strongly protested and argued that "if at this stage Mahatma Gandhi left the Congress, it would have a very unfortunate effect on the public and the Congress would not emerge successful in the elections.[3]

The elections were envisaged under the Government of India Act 1935 which came into force on 2nd July, 1935

1. Sitaramayya, *op. cit.*, I. p. 942.
2. Rajput *op. cit.*, pp. 132-33.
3. Iyer, *op. cit.*, pp. 77-78.

providing for provincial autonomy and a federal government at the centre. Inspite of their opposition to the Act both the Congress and the League decided to contest the provincial elections. The Congress Working Committee at its meeting on 7th July, 1936 appointed a Parliamentary Sub-committee consisting of Maulana Azad, Rajendra Prasad and Sardar Patel which was given the responsibility and intricate task of guiding the Congress ministries in different provinces.[1]

The elections were held early in 1937. During the election campaign the Congress and the League had co-operated to some extent notably in the United Provinces where they developed an understanding that coalition government would be formed.[2] The results proved that neither the Congress nor the League could claim to represent Muslims. However the success of the Congress in the general constituencies proved its popularity on the all India level. This moment of opportunity, however, brought with it the need to make a vital decision. Should the Congress form a coalition with the Muslim League ? The Muslim League had failed to capture a majority of the Muslim votes. Nor was it in a position to form a government on its own in any province. This realisation lay behind the almost conciliatory posture taken up by Jinnah soon after the elections. In a public statement Jinnah declared, "nobody will welcome an honourable settlement between the Hindus and the Muslims more than I and nobody will be more ready to help it."[3] On 1st March, 1937 he again expressed Muslims League's willingness to co-operate with any group or party if the basic principles are determined by common consent.[4]

Encouraged by the amicable manner in which the elections had been contested by both the Congress and the League,[5] Khaliquzzaman, leader of the Provincial Muslim

---

1. Rajput *op. cit.*, pp. 141-42.
2. Mishael Brecher, *Jawaharlal Nehru—A Political Biography*, London, 1959, p. 231.
3. B. Shiva Rao, *Farming of India's Constitution—A study* Nasik 1968, p. 22.
4. *The Leader*, 1st March, 1937.
5. Khaliquzzaman, *Pathway to Pakistan*, Lahore, 1961, p. 153.

League Parliamentary Board started discussions with Govind Ballabh Pant, Primer designate, soon after the elections. In fact Khaliquzzaman had spurned an offer to join the government headed by Nawab of Chhatari who was invited by the British to form an interim government.[1] Pant is reported to have offered the League two seats in a possible Congress Ministry[2] and earned the displeasure of Jawahar lal Nehru.[3] When Maulana Azad went to Lucknow on 12th July, 1937 in order to form the Congress Ministry he met Khaliquzzaman and Nawab Ismail Khan both of whom assured him not only to co-operate with the Congress but also to support the Congress programme. In return Maulana Azad held out hope that both would be taken into the Government. When Maulana Azad reached Allahabad he learnt that Jawaharlal Nehru had already written to Khaliquzzaman and Nawab Ismail Khan that only one of them could be taken into the Ministry. Maulana Azad thought that the local position was such that neither of them could enter the Ministry alone. Both of them, therefore declined to accept Jawahar Lal Nehru's offer.[4] The Congress decision against coalition with the League appeared to be logical and theoretically correct but there is a broad consensus of well informed opinion that in practice the decion proved disastrous.[5]

In U.P., the Congress enjoyed absolute majority but it was not so in Assam. Maulana Azad, therefore, did not approve of forming a ministry in Assam but with the support of Subhas Chandra Bose, the Congress President, as also of Sardar Patel, Congress ministry was formed in Assam but soon afterwards it was confronted with a crisis which

1. Reforms Office, F. No: 891/ 40R. Note by Donaldson dated 14th August, 1940,
2. Haig to Linlithgow 7th April, 1937 Haig Correspondence vol. 17A.
3. Nehru to Pant 30th March, 1937 AICC File. No. 1. 1936-37.
4. Maulana Azad *op. cit.*, pp. 170-71.
5. Munshi, *op. cit.*, p. 48.

Gopinath Bardoloi, Primer of Assam, communicated over the phone to Maulana Azad who, along with Subhas Chandra Bose, proceeded to Shilong on 14th September, 1938 and succeeded in resolving the crisis by forming a coalition ministry with five Hindu and three Muslim ministers (7).

Assumption of office by the Congress in September, 1937 provided the Muslim League an opportunity to stir up Muslim opinion against the alleged communal bias of Congress governments. The League could not challenge the Congress on political issues publicly to any great extent, perhaps because election had proved the appeal of the Congress stand on those issues. Instead the League sought to embrass Congress governments by alleging that they were unwilling to safeguard the religious and cultural rights of the Muslims. Opposition to the flag and Bande Matram manifested itself in various parts of the country. Sometimes issues of a very trivial nature sparked off a communal controversy and the case of Bihar showed that an indecisive government complicated the communal problem. The Muslim League in Bhagalpur took advantage of a suggestion in the Provincial Legislative Assembly that the custom be the guiding principle regarding processions before mosques and the right to slaughter cows.[1] On 29th October, 1938 Maulana Azad sent a telegram to Rajendra Prasad informing him that he had to postpone his journey owing to indisposition and desired him to decide Bhagalpur-Gaya affairs removing Muslim complaints which have perturbed Muslim nationalists (8).

What provided an opportunity to Muslim League to accuse the Congress of insincerity and communalism was somewhat conservative attitude of the Congress to tenancy legislation in Bengal and Bihar in contrast to its radical policy in U.P. In Orissa a Tenancy Amendment Bill was introduced in the Assembly but in the meanwhile the Congress Parliamentary Board received complaints against Biswanath Das, Premier of Orissa. In order to go through the complaints

1. Anita Inder Singh, *op. cit.*, p. 37.

Rajendra Prasad was to proceed to Cuttuck but he could not do so because of ill health. Nor was Maulana Azad in a position to go to Cuttuck. He, therefore, asked Biswanath Das to meet him at Calcutta on 1st January, 1939 to discuss the Orissa Tenancy Amendment Bill. He also summoned the dissident Congress leaders Nillakantha Das, Godavarish Misra to Calcutta to look into the allegations against the Premier of Orista (9).

When Maulana Azad was trying to resolve Orissa ministerial crisis, the Congress itself was torn as under by the struggle waged by Subhas Chandra Bose at Tripuri to retain its presidentship, despite Mahatma Gandhi's dissatisfaction with his leadership. Thirteen members of the working Committee resigned in protest in February, 1939. Subhas Chandra Bose tried to lead the Congress alone but his health broke down. He could not attend the fifty-second session of the Congress held at Tripura on 10th March, 1939. Maulana Azad presided over the meeting where Govind Ballabh Pant moved a resolution requesting the re-elected president to nominate the Working Committee in ocordance with the wishes of Mahatma Gandhi who alone could lead the country to victory during a crisis.[1] Driven to desperation Subhas Chandra Bose sought the assistance of Mahatma Gandhi who simply ignored him. Jawaharlal Nehru tried to mediate but in vain.

It was about this time that Maulana Azad met with an accident and fractured his leg. Jawaharlal Nehru personally looked after him during his stay at Allahabad. Referring to this incident Maulana Azad observed, "When I think of my accident at Allahabad, I find that nothing more could have been done for my comfort and treatment by my own people here had it happened in Calcutta. Indeed the nearest and dearest of my relatives could not have felt more than you did for me there. I do not know how to express my feelings of gratitude to you. Believe me, my heart is extremely grateful for your love and kindness" (11).

---

1. *The Indian Annual Register*, III 1939, p. 332.

Even in his sick-bed at Calcutta, Maulana Azad was exercised over the crisis the Congress was confronted with. In his letter of 17th April, 1939 he wrote to Jawaharlal Nehru, "I do not know whether you have seen the letter of Subhas to Gandhiji It is a pity that Subhas Babu is exactly in the position where he was before Tripuri and there is no hope that he will improve the situation by acting on the Tripuri resolution. On the one hand he calls the Pant Resolution against the constitution and *ultra vires,* on the other he wants Gandhiji to accept certain conditions. Along with this he does not hesitate in making the extravagant assertion that the Pant Resolution would have been lost had the Socialist group not become neutral . . . . I consider the affair of Subhas Babu to be neither a struggle between the right and the left, nor the question of composite and homogeneous Working Committee. It is only a matter of Subhas and some of his supporters. It matters little in what form the tangle comes to an end. We have to consider these questions independently and specifically in order to reach a solution"(11).

The internal dissensions of the Congress became so acute that Subhas Chandra Bose was forced to resign on 29th April, 1939 and Rajendra Prasad was elected Congress President in his place. Subhas Chandra Bose formed Forward Block Party devoted to the revolutionary struggle for freedom. Rajendra Prasad selected his own Working Committee of which Maulana Azad was a member. He could not attend the meeting of the All India Congress Committee held at Bombay on 24th-27th June, 1939 due to the slow progress of recovery. He wanted to discuss many things about the present and the future with Jawaharlal Nehru but had to postpone the same till after the latter's return from Ceylon. Jawaharlal Nehru was deputed by the Congress Working Committee to go to Ceylon to compose the differences between the Indian imigrants and the Ceylonese (12).

In the meanwhile trouble was brewing in the Punjab where the Congress was losing ground in the rural areas. When the Alienation of Land (Third Amendment) Bill was introduced by the Unionist Ministry, the Congress remained neutral. While agriculturists of all communities supported the

Bill, the Hindu non-agriculturist and money-lending classes were up in arms. The Congress Working Committee asked the Congress Parliamentary Party to support the measure. Non-agricultural members of the Punjab Congress were unhappy over these instructions in as much as they did not want to lose the support of the non-agriculturist and commercial classes who financed their party. Maulana Azad had already reminded them of their duty to give full and unstinted support to all legislation to ameliorate condition of the masses.[1]

In order to solve the Punjab tangle Rajendra Prasad, Congress President, sought the advice of Maulana Azad who in his letter of 10th July, 1939 observed, "The Punjab affairs need our immediate attention but you are right in saying that they can not be settled unless a strong man goes there. So far as I am concerned, I am yet unable to use my leg. If someone has to go there immediately, I think either you yourself, Sardar Patel or Pandit Jawaharlal Nehru should go. Jawaharlal is going to Ceylon, and he will not be able to return before August. Now the matter devolves on you or Patel. The malady of the Punjab is chronic and deep-seated. It will not be sufficient to glean at the surface only. The real causes of the disease are to be diagnosed and firm steps are to be taken to root out the disease absolutely"(13).

In view of Maulana Azad's inability to attend the Congress Working Committee meeting at Wardha on 9th-12th August, 1939 Rajendra Prasad and Sardar Patel insisted on inviting Maulana Azad's opinion in respect of the case of Subhas Chandra Bose. Maulana Azad, therefore, sent his opinion in writing to Rajendra Prasad to the effect that the attitude of Subhas Babu was wrong and it was necessary for the Working Committee to express its opinion. But he had suggested not to show too much strictness on this occasion. Thinking that Jawaharlal Nehru would take part in consideration of this matter, Maulana Azad talked to him over the phone but Jawaharlal Nehru remained practically aloof and

---

1. Anita Inder Singh, *op. cit.*, p. 43.

the decision was taken by the Working Committee in the absence of his agreement (14).

While the Congress Working Committee was delibrating over the crisis created by Subhas Chandra Bose there was a tension in the international affairs and the danger of the outbreak of World War II was felt all over the world. Perceiving the impending danger, Maulana Azad sent a telegram from Lucknow on 27th August, 1939 to Rajendra Prasad to call an emergency meeting of the Working Committee to consider the critical situation (15). When Britain entered the World War II in Europe Lord Linlithgow, Viceroy of India declared India a beligerent without, consulting the representatives of the Indian political parties. This naturally aroused wide spread public protest. On 5th September, 1939 Maulana Azad and Jawaharlal Nehru issued a joint statement which, among other things, pointed out that, "the hand of friendship the Congress had extended to the British people in this hour of world crisis has been spurned by their Government. How far that Government represents them, it is for them to say, but we have to consider the Viceroy's statement as England's reply to India" (70).

The Viceroy was profoundly moved by Mahatma Gandhi's sympathy for England and he hoped that the Mahatma would be able to keep things on the right line at the Congress Working Committee meeting especially on the matter of defence liaison.[1] Maulana Azad sent a telegram on 5th September, 1939 to Rajendra Prasad asking him to end indefinitness and convene the meeting of the Congress Working Committee (18). Subsequently the Congress Working Committee met at Wardha from 8th to 15th September 1939 and expressed its displeasure at the flouting of the Indian opinion by the British Government. Mahatma Gandhi was alone in suggesting unconditional support for the British on a non-violent basis.

While the Congress Working Committee was busy discussing the war crisis, Sir Stafford Cripps visited Wardha to win

---

1. Anita Inder Singh, *op. cit.*, p. 46.

over Indian participation in the war. According to him the British Government would make an immediate declaration that with the cessation of hostilities, India would be declared independent forthwith. The declaration would also include a clause that India would be free to decide whether to remain within the British Commonwealth or not. For the duration of the war, the Executive Council would be reconstituted and members would have the status of Ministers. The position of the Viceroy would be that of a constitutional head.[1]

The Congress Working Committee resolved that the issue of war and peace must be decided by the Indian people and no outside authority can impose this decision upon them. Nor can Indian people permit their resources to be exploited for imperialist ends. It also invited the British Government to declare in unequivocal terms what their war aims were. The Working Committee appointed a War Committee consisting of Jawaharlal Nehru (Chairman), Maulana Azad and Sardar Patel to deal with the question in connection with the changing war situation.[2]

The British Government's failure to define their political objectives led to a deadlock. In fact the British Government exploited Congress-League differences as an excuse to avoid political advance.[3] This led to the Congress Working Committee on 30th October, 1939 to order the Congress ministries to resign. Soon after the resignation of the Congress ministries Maulana Azad and Jawaharlal Nehru met Mahatma Gandhi and Rajendra Prasad at Delhi and there was an indication of a political agreement between the Congress and the League for the settlement of India's immediate political difficulties. Subsequently a proposal to that effect was submitted by Rajendra Prasad on behalf of the Congress and by Jinnah on behalf of the League.[4] The Viceroy asked the Congress and the League to reconstruct the provincial Government and to

---

1. Maulana Azad, *op. cit*, p. 47.
2. A.M. Zaidi, *The Encyclopaedia of Indian National Congress*, XII, New Delhi, 1981, pp. 194-97.
3. *National Herald*, 26th October 1939.
4. Iyer, *op. cit.*, p. 102.

join the Viceroy's Executive Council but the talks failed because the Congress insisted upon the approval of the Government to the framing of the future constitution of India by a constituent assembly elected by Indians.

Consequent upon failure of the talks, the Viceroy published the correspondence that passed between him and Maulana Azad. Maulana Azad, therefore, issued a statement which, among other things, clarified that "the real, difficulties are not communal but political. The British Government are not yet prepared to concede the right of self-determination to India in practice, however much it may proclaim it in theory to the world. We put its professions to a test. Let us have a right to frame our own constitution and we shall do it. We failed in the past in assisting the British Government to frame a constitution for us. But helping the British Government to frame a constitution for India is some thing very different from independently framing a constitution for ourselves with certainty that the constitution will be accepted and enforced. The two principal organisations of which the Viceroy made reference in his Statement, the Indian National Congress and the All India Muslim League, both declared that they aim at independence for India and, so far as I know, there is no party or group in India which does not want full powers for India to manage her own affairs by whatever name or expression that freedom may be called or described. There is this fundamental unity in all parties in India and this is a universal urge of all Indians which the Congress emodied in its demand for a clear declaration" (71).

In the meanwhile the coalition ministry in Assam was confronted with a crisis. Of the eight Ministers only two were Congress men. The six non-Congress Ministers were naturally averse to leave the Ministry. In the words of Gopinath Bardoloi, Premier of Assam, "Congress circles themselves, and some Congress office-holders too, are supporting them." However Bardoloi himself had assured Maulana Azad that he would resign by 12th November, 1939 (18). Fazlul Huq, Premier of Bengal, had gone one step further. He had already promised the British unconditional support for the war effort against the wishes of Jinnah and was simultaneously engaged in his intermittent 'filtrations' with the Congress.[1] When Maulana Azad came to know about these developments, he wrote to Jawaharlal Nehru on 11th November, 1939, "Fazlul Huq had said in reply to your statement that he would inform you on reaching Calcutta. More than a week has already passed. Please wire to him immediately that you are waiting for his information so that you may chalk out your programme accordingly. A copy of this telegram should also be given to the press. Your reply had absolutely upset Fazlul Huq. All his colleagues are blaming him for his folly. This is the most opportune time to bring him to his senses by persistently forcing the issues at him so that the absurdity may end for all time to come and the public should not get a chance of forgetting this episode"(18).

Taking full advantage of Muslim grievances against the Congress Provincial Governments, the League had become a force in Indian politics by the time the Congress ministries resigned. Jinnah called on the League to observe 22nd December 1939 as Deliverance Day which passed off quietly in most places but it naturally infuriated Congress leaders. The statement of Jinnah about the Deliverance Day created an embrassing situation for Jawaharlal Nehru who was to resume talks with him in Bombay. His distrust of Jinnah by now was so deep as to make all unity talks useless. He wrote to Jinnah and asked him if there was some common ground for discussions to yield fruit. Jinnah replied that no common ground was possible "so long as the Congress is not prepared to treat the Muslim League as the authoritative and representative organisation of the Musalmans of India." The preliminary condition emphasised by Jinnah involved repudiation by the Congress of all those Muslims who were not in the League. "There were" replied Jawaharlal Nehru "a large number of Muslims in the Congress who have been and are our closest colleagues."[2]

---

1. Anita Inder Singh, *op. cit.*, pp. 46, 55.
2. Zaidi, *op. cit.*, XII pp. 262-63.

Soon afterwards Maulana Azad was elected Congress President on 18th February, 1940 by an overwhelming majority.[1] On 27th February, 1940, Maulana Azad sent a telegram to Rajendra Prasad informing him that he was leaving Calcutta for Patna with Mahatma Gandhi by Delhi Express (22). The Congress Working Committee which met at Patna from 28th February to 1st March discussed the possibility of Civil Disobedience as soon as organization permitted and circumstance demanded. The fifty third session of the Congress held at Ramgarh in Bihar on 19th-20th March, 1940 under the presidentship of Maulana Azad reaffirmed the Patna resolution. The Congress could not be a party to the war without British guarantees for independence and a Constituent Assembly where the rights of minorities would be protected by agreement between the representatives of various communities.[2] In his presidential address at Ramgarh session Maulana Azad referred to India's stand with the democratic powers and said, "India cannot endure the prospect of Nazism and Fascism but she is even more tired of British imperialism. If India remains deprived of her natural right to freedom, this would clearly mean that British Imperialism continued to flourish with all its traditional characteristics and under such conditions India would on no account be prepared to lend helping hand for the triumphs of British Imperialism.[3] Elaborating his concepts of composite nationalism and pluralistic religious co-existence he declared, "As a Musalman I have a special interest in Islamic religion and culture and I cannot tolerate any interference with them. But in addition to these sentiments, I have others also which the realities and conditions of my life have forced upon me. The spirit of Islam does not come in the way of these sentiments; it guides and helps me forward. I am proud of being an Indian. I am a part of the indivisible unity that is Indian nationality. I am indispensible to this noble edifice and without me this splendid structure

1. Iyer, *op. cit.*, p. 104.
2. *Iudian Annual Register*, Vol. I, 1940, p. 218.
3. Zaidi, *op. cit.*, XII. p. 346.

of India is incomplete. I am an essential element which has gone to build India. I can never surrender the claim."[1]

This presidential address originally written in Urdu was translated into English by no less a person than Jawaharlal Nehru. Admiring his English version Maulana Azad wrote, "Translation, in a way, is much more difficult than composing in original. It is by no means easy to maintain the literary content of the original writing and at the same time convey through translation the literary style of the writer. Only a person with equal command over both the languages could have attempted such a task. What particularly strikes me in your translation is the fact that no feature of the original has suffered through it and you have conveyed my Urdu literary style so successfully in English that I should not be surprised if it occurs to the reader that the original was English and not Urdu" (25).

Congratulating Maulana Azad on his election, Vijayaraghavachariar, former Congress President, wrote, "You know that there are various views about what our unhappy country wants now. I always remember your double formula. I can not any time think of you without it; the same time remembering the formula truely original and so suitable to the condition of India.[2] In reply Maulana Azad wrote, "our destination is still far and the way is beset with wearisome obstacles. Nevertheless we must have to keep marching on. We are not to see whether we have gained the destination but to continue on the journey in quest unfailingly. The saying of a Persian poet is always on my lips:

The pilgrim of love can never face failure;
Because the very keeping on the pilgrimage is in itself the greatest success" (30).

The Ramgarh Congress unequivocally declared that freedom could not exist within the orbit of British rule and the Congress could not be a party to the war without British guarantees for a Constituent Assembly based on adult

1. Zaidi, *op. cit.*, p. 364.
2. Iyer; *op. cit.*, p. 104.

sufferage. Soon afterwards Mahatma Gandhi launched his Individual Satyagraha campaign as a symbolic gesture of protest. The political statement thus created worried Jinnah who sulked at the British refusal to break with Mahatma Gandhi.[1] Muslim Leaguers themselves were urging Jinnah to define the party's goals.[2] Some even suggested a Congress-League pact.[3]

It was against this political background that the League at its Lahore session on 23rd March 1940 passed its Pakistan Resolution which declared that no constitutional plan would be acceptable to Muslims unless "geographically contiguous units are demarcated into regions which should be so constituted, with such territorial readjustments as may be necessary that the areas in which the Muslims are numerically in a majority, as in the North-Western and Eastern zones of India, should be so grouped to constitute independent states in which the constituent units shall be autonomous and sovereign."[4] The Pakistan Resolution deeply hurt Mahatma Gandhi who denounced it as a call for the vivesection of India. He declared, "partition means a patent untruth.My whole soul rebels against the idea that Hinduism and Islam represent two antagunistic cultures and doctrines."[5] In order to take stock of the political situation Maulana Azad called the Congress Working Committee at Wardha and asked Acharya J.B. Kripalani, Congress Secretary, to send additional invitations to Pattabhi Sitaramayya, Dr. B.C. Roy and Master Tara Singh (24). The Congress Working Committee held on 16th-19th April, 1940 gave consideration to the situation in the country as it has developed since the Ramgarh Congress and to the necessity for preparing the Congress organisation for Satyagraha which the Ramgarh Congress declaried was in-

1. Anita Inder Singh,*op. cit.*, p. 55.
2. *National Herald*, 20th February, 1940.
3. *National Herald*, 26th February, 1940.
4. S.S. Pirzada (ed) *Foundation of Pakistan : All India Muslim League Documents* vol. II (1924-47) Karachi, 1970 p. 341.
5. *Harijan*, 13th April, 1940.

evitable in future.[1] In order to bolster its single nation theory, the Congress decided to observe National Week throughout the country with more than usual enthusiasm this year. Maulana Azad issued an appeal saying, "If we imbibe the true spirit of the Constructive Programme, I have no hesitation in affirming that every atom of this land will respond to the call of national life. But do we expect to carry warmth to others if our hearths grow cold? No, we must kindle our own fires first. The National Week provides us with that opportunity" (72).

Early in April, 1940 Lord Zetland, Secretary of State for India, announced that negotiation and no dictation was embodied in the undertaking given by His Majesty's Government to examine constitutional field in consultation with representatives of all parties and interests in India. In response to this announcement Mahatma Gandhi declared that he would do nothing "to embrass" Great Britain although the Congress could not lend its moral influence to England.[2] On 18th April 1940 Lord Zetland stated in the House of Lords that agreement among Indian communities was essential if the vision of a united India was to become a reality and added that the British could not force a constitution on the Muslims.[3] In response to this speech Maulana Azad, issued a statement on 22nd April 1940 and declared "Every difficulty that the Secretary of State raises is completely met by the proposed Constituent Assembly. Only such an Assembly can deal with problems relating to Hindus and Muslims and the Indian states" (17) but the British Government chose to ignore the nationalist public opinion which was opposed to partirion of India. Maulana Azad and Khan Bahadur Allah Bakhsh organised at Delhi an All India Independent Muslim Conference which denounced partition of India and repudiated the Muslim League's elaim that they were the sole representatives of the Muslims of India.[4]

---

1. Zaidi, *op cit.*, XII, p. 423.
2. *The Incian Year Book*, XVIII, 1941-42, pp. 887-88.
3. Anita Inder Singh, *op cit.*, pp. 58-59.
4. Iyer, *op. cit.*, p. 110.

Events, however, were moving fast in Europe. V.K. Krishna Menon during his long stay in London had cultivated Members of the Labour Party. He used to send to Jawaharlal Nehru all kinds of proposals for securing the help of interests friendly to India. On 21st April, 1940 Jawaharlal Nehru recommended to Maulana Azad one such scheme of Krishna Menon for visiting America in order to explain the Indian situation to the Americans. Maulana Azad in his reply to Jawahrlal Nehru wrote on 24th April, 1940, "I agree with you that if Krishna Menon goes to America on his own accord, it would be useful to the demand of the time to some extent. Had it come before us previous to the meeting of the Working Committee, it would have been decided in it. However, I am writing to the General Secretary to send £ 100 immediately to him. You say that I should write a letter to him also. I think that if I write to him as the President, it would necessarily mean that he is going there on behalf of the Congress and as you yourself write, it would be against expediency to carry the matter to such an extent. It would be better if you write him a letter saying, "I am glad to hear that you are going to America. I hope your presence there would enable them to understand the existing Indian situation" (27).

The German invasion of Holland and Belgium on 10th May, 1940 exposed Britain to a possible German attack. England resisted the Axis single handed and this fact was atleast partly responsible for a changed role for India in the imperial defence machine. In the meanwhile Zetland was replaced by L.S. Amery as Secretary of State for India. On 23rd May, 1940 Amery reiterated the British Government's intention that India should attain full and equal partnership in the British Commonwealth of Nations. Maulana Azad immediately issued a statement on 25th May, 1940 at Nainital, "It is to be regretted that there is not the slightest shadow of a change in the angle of vision of the British Cabinet about India".[1]

1. *The Indian Annual Register* II, 1940, p. 75.

There were conflicting views in the Congress camp with regard to the question of participation in the War effort. Mahatma Gandhi did not want to "embrass" Great Britain. Jawaharlal Nehru thought that it was against the dignity of India to take advantage of the weakness of England by launching *Satyagraha* at that critical juncture. In a letter to Rajendra Prasad he wrote, "The *Satyagraha* is not immediately indicated even if we were ready for it. I think it would be wrong for us at this particular moment when Britain is in peril, to take advantage of her distress and rush at its throat."[1] Maulana Azad held diametrically opposite view. In his letter dated 25th May, 1940 to Jawaharlal Nehru he stated, "I absolutely fail to grasp this mode of thinking. In fact this very method is totally wrong that we should first formulate conclusions about our line of action. I do not know what is the "*shaan*" of India. I only want to know what is the considered decision, and where does it lead to ? Nothing can be more absurd than to chalk out a way and then refuse to tread upon it. We gave Britain fullest opportunity to take us with her but she stubbornly refused to do so. We were forced to decide not to participate in this Imperialistic War. Is our present stand such that it "embrasses" her (in the words of Gandhiji) or in your words it is against the "*shaan*" of India, there can be no remedy to it. We are not responsible for it. It lies with the imprudent vanity of the British Government. I do not understand how this confused and illogical conception could find a way to your mind. You, least of all, are not expected to think in such a way." (29)

In order to reconcile these conflicting views, Maulana Azad called the Congress Working Committee and asked Kripalani, General Secretary, to send special invitations to Acharya Narendra Deo, Achyut Patwardhan, Dr. Pattabhi Sitaramayyah and Mrs. Vijay Lakshmi Pandit (31). The Congress Working Committee met at Wardha on 17th-21st

---

1. Chaudhary, Valmiki, ed. Rajendra Prasad: *Correspondence and Select Documents* V, New Delhi, 1984, p. 3.

June, 1940 under Maulana Azad's presidentship and after five days deliberations came to the conclusion that "they are unable to go the full length with Gandhiji. But they recognise that he should be free to pursue his great ideal in his own way and therefore absolve him from responsibility for the programme and activity which the Congress has to pursue under the conditions at present prevailing in India and the world in regard to external aggression and internal disorder."[1]

In the meanwhile the fall of France produced in India a new feeling in favour of Britain. Mahatma Gandhi declared "we do not seek our independence out of Britain's ruin" and Jawaharlal Nehru proclaimed, "England's difficulty is not India's opportunity."[2] In order to discuss political situation in the country Maulana Azad called Congress Working Committee which met at Delhi on 3rd-7th July, 1940 and resolved "the acknowledgement by Great Britain of the complete independence of India is the only solution of the problem facing both India and Britain and are, therefore, of opinion that such an unequivocal declaration should be immediately made and that as an immediate step in giving effect to it, a provisional National Government should be constituted at the centre, which, though formed as a transitory measure, should be such as to command the confidence of all the elected elements in the Central Legislature, and secure, the closest co-operation of the responsible government in the provinces if these measures are adopted it will enable the Congress to throw its full weight in the efforts for the effective organisation of the defence of the country.[3]

At this meeting of the Working Committee, Khan Abdul Ghaffar Khan reported that the British Government had refused permission to the deputation of the Provincial Congress Committee to visit Waziristan and to render them such aid for their social welfare as possible. The Congress Working Committee, therefore, deputed Bholabhai Desai and

1. Zaidi, *op. cit.*, XII. p. 427.
2. *The Indian Year Book*, XXVII, 1941-42, pp. 887-88.
3. Zaidi, *op. cit.*, XII, p. 429.

Asaf Ali to proceed to Waziristan to carry on the work that the provincial deputation would have done. In his statement to the press Maulana Azad said, "It has long been our declared policy and desire to have friendly relations with our neighbour nations and peoples and we are convinced that when we have the chance, we shall be able to do so with advantage to all concerned. A free India will be strong enough to protect her frontiers but the real strength that we seek to build is the friendship of our Border peoples." (74)

Similarly when the British Government closed the Burma-China Road, Maulana Azad protested and said, "the closing of the Burma road means a severe restriction on these growing contacts and flouting of Indian opinion. It is in complete conflict with the foreign policy which the people of India desire to pursue. It is a violation of international usage as well as of Sino-British treaties and is evidently meant to hamper China in her struggle for freedom. It's greatest significance lies in the light it throws on British policy which claims to do one thing in Europe and follows an entirely different course in India and China." (76)

The resolution adopted at the Delhi meeting of the All India Congress Committee created some misunderstanding. On 11th July 1940 Maulana Azad issued a statement and said, "it was wrong to say that the Congress had only shown its readiness to defend India and not participate or help in the War. When we passed the resolution every one of us was quite clear on this point that if India's demands were fulfilled it will be the duty of Indians to participate in the War.[1] Since this statement was misunderstood by Jawaharlal Nehru, Maulana Azad clarified the position in his letter of 19th July, 1940 stating, "please re-read my statement. I did not say that the resolution was unanimously passed. I have only explained the mental aspect of the resolution saying that all were clear in their 'minds' that in case the Indian demand is accepted she (India) would participate in the War". (32) In the same letter

---

1. S. Gopal (ed). *Selected Works of Jawaharlal Nehru*, XI, (1978), New Delhi p. 76 n. 2.

he requested Jawaharlal Nehru not to issue any statement in this regard till they met at the ensuing session of the All India Congress Committee at Poona.

The All India Congress Committee met at Poona on 23rd-28th July, 1940 under the presidentship of Maulana Azad. Before commencing the proceedings he made a statement explaining the two official resolutions as also the circumstances leading to the meeting of the All India Congress Committee. The first resolution declared that while the Congress must continue to adhere strictly to the principle of non-violence in the struggle for independence, it was unable in the then prevailing circumstances to declare that the principle should be extended to free India's national defence. The second resolution demanded complete independence of India which would "enable the Congress to throw its full weight in to the efforts for the effective organisation of the country". The All India Congress Committee passed both the resolutions by an over whelming majority.[1] In his opening remarks Maulana Azad observed, "There is not a soul in the Congress who is not anxious to go the whole length with Mahatma Gandhi if he can help it but we cannot close our eyes to hard facts. We know that arms and amunitions have not been able to save the freedom of France, Holland, Belgium and Norway but we also know that human nature even after realising the futility of armed resistence is not prepared to give up force. Honestly we cannot go as far as Mahatma Gandhi wants us to go. We admit that it is a weakness on our part but it is a weakness which we share with the entire humanity. Though we cannot go with Mahatma Gandhi the whole hog we do not wish to stop him from pursuing his own path." (75) Maulana Azad stated at the press conference at Bombay on 31st July, 1940 that the Congress had tried its utmost to retain Mahatma Gandhi's leadership but had failed. He said that, "if Mahatma Gandhi's leadership was not available to the next struggle, if

1. Zaidi, *op. cit.*, XII, p. 374.

it became necessary, the Congress should herself shoulder the responsibility of leadership."[1]

When the Congress camp was in disarray, Maulana Azad received a letter dated 4th August, 1940 from Lord Linlithgow stating, "I have been authorised to invite a certain number of representative Indians to join my Executive Council. I have been authorised further to establish a War Advisory Council which will meet at intervals and which would contain representatives of the Indian States and of other interest in the national life of India as a whole". This letter sent from Ooty was recieved by Maulana Azad on 7th August 1940 and it was on the following day that this offer was made public by the Viceroy. This offer is known as "August offer". On 8th August, 1940 Maulana Azad sent a telegram to the Viceroy stating, "I would have readily availed of preasure of meeting Your Excellency but when His Majesty's Government have already thought fit to announce a definite line of action may I ask how far there still remains a chance of usefulness of further discussion." (34)

The Viceroy responded by telegram dated 10th August, 1940 stating "policy of His Majesty's Government is set out in my statement and it is my hope that within its terms the Indian National Congress will...feel able to join me in the Central Government and in the War Advisory Council. I shall be glad to see you."[2] In reply Maulana Azad sent a telegram on the same day declaring, "I do not find any meeting ground for Congress in the terms of the declaration of August eight. Apart from other fundamental questions there is not even any suggestion for national government." (35)

In order to consider the Vicerory's latest pronouncement on India's political advance, Maulana Azad called at Wardha the Congress Working Committee which met on 18th-23rd August, 1940. In his interim reply dated 19th August 1940 Maulana Azad said, "The Working Committee will express their views in the course of the next few days dealing

---

1. *Indian Annual Register*, V, Pt. II, 1940, p. 11.
2. *Ibid*; p. 201.

ing with this master more fully but meanwhile, I may inform you that the Committee have read the statements embodying the British Government's decisions and attitude in regard to India with deep regret."(37) The Congress Working Committee came to the conclusion *inter alia*, that "the statement referrred to are wholly opposed not only to the principle of democracy as acclaimed by the British Government in the War but also to the best interests of India and they can not be a party to accepting the proposals contained in the statement or advising the country to accept them. The Working Committee consider that these declarations and offers not only fall far short of the Congress demand but would be impediments to the evolutions of a free and united India."[1]

In order to take stock of the political situation in the country, Maulana Azad called All India Congress Committee which met at Bombay on 15th-16th September, 1940. Before starting the proceedings he observed, "The British Government had left no alternative for us but to take the next step and these events made us to decide to again request Mahatma Gandhi to assume the active leadership of the Congress". It adopted the following resolution, "The Congress is pledged under Mr. Gandhi's leadership to non-violence for the vindication of India's freedom. At this grave crisis in the movement for national, freedom, All India Congress Committee request him to guide in the action that should be taken. The Congress Working Committee which met at Bombay on 13th-17th September, 1940 under the presidentship of Maulana Azad resolved, "In view of the resolution just passed by the All India Congress Committee, the Congress Working Committee calls upon all Congress organisations to stop all Civil Disobedience, individual or other, pending definite instructions from Gandhiji. He regards this suspension as indispensable for his forthcoming interview with His Excellency the Viceroy".

Mahatma Gandhi met the Vicerory at Simla on 27th and

1. Zaidi. *op. cit.*, XII, p. 435.

30th September, 1940 but the talks failed.[1] In a press interview Maulana Azad said, "I admit that the outcome of the Simla meeting is not contrary to expectations. The very presence of the British Government in India indicates one reality, from whatever angle we see the denial of free will of India. Naturally therefore, we can not expect her to tolerate the free expression of our decision about the War even if it be of purely non-violent nature."(77) It was at the instance of Mahatma Gandhi that the Congress Working Committee met at Wardha on 11th-13th October, 1940 and listened to an account of his talks with the Vicerory. It approved of what he had done and repeated the instructions given to the Congress men by the All India Congress Committee at its last meeting in Bombay that they should give him the fullest co-operations possible in all he might require or expected them to do. As desired by Mahatma Gandhi the Individual *Satyagraha* was started on 17th October, 1940. On 26th November, 1940 Maulana Azad reiterated at Lahore that "he was personally in favour of Mass Civil Disobedience but since they had entrusted everything to Mr. Gandhi, they must carry out the Mahatma's Programme."[2] In the course of an interview at Lahore on 30th December, 1940 Maulana Azad observed, "If India is invaded tomorrow and there is no other alternative to defend my country, I will not hesitate to take arms and fight."[3] Subsequently he was arrested on 3rd January, 1941 at the Allahabad Railway station while he was on his way from Delhi to Calcutta and was sentenced 18 months simple imprisonment in Naini Jail under the Defence of India Rules for delivering a prejudicial speech at Allahabad.[4]

While Maulana Azad and other *Satyagrahis* were in jail, the Congress Right got frustrated by the political impasse and discussed possibility of returning to office. Prominent among such Congress leaders were Rajagopalachari and Bholabhai

1. Zaidi, *op. cit.*, XII pp. 444-45.
2. *The Indian Annual Register* II, 1940, p. 47.
3. *Ibid* , p. 51.
4. Iyer, *op. cit.*, pp. 125-26.

Desai who had lost confidence in *Satyagraha* and wanted the Congress to resume parliamentry activities.[1] On the other hand the arrest of Subhas Chandra Bose and the banning of his Forward Block Party revived the terrorist movement in Bengal. Subhas Chandra Bose himself escaped house-arrest on the eve of his trial in 1941 and journeyed in disguise to Afghanistan. He flew from Kabul to Moscow and then Berlin where he was welcomed by Hitler who gave him high powered radio facilities to beam daily broadcasts to India urging his compatriots to rise in revolt against British tyranny.

In Europe events were moving fast. Norway, Denmark, Holland and Belgium were runover in Hitler blitzkrieg. With the fall of France and its capitulation, England stood alone to carry on the fight. When Hitler failed to subdue England, he invaded Soviet Russia on 22nd June, 1941. The Japanese attack on pearl Harbour on 6th December, 1941 forced USA to enter into what became a global war. In order to test Congress reaction to this changed war situation the British Government released Maulana Azad and Jawaharlal Nehru in the first wek eof December, 1941. Mahatma Gandhi issued a statement at Wardha, "The only meaning I can attach to the release therefore is that the Government of India expects the prisoners to have changed their opinion regarding their self invited soltitude....I am hoping that the Government of India will soon be disillusioned". About the future programme of the Congress he stated that it was left to the Congress President "to consider whether and when to call the Congress Working Committee or the AICC, the two bodies will determine the future policy of the Congress."[2] Maulana Azad decided to call the meeting of the Congress Working Committee at Bardoli. On 11th December, 1941 he sent a telegram to Jawaharlal Nehru stating, "starting seventeenth direct Bombay, please accompany nineteenth morning." (40) On 18th December, 1941 Maulana Azad was interviewed by the press at Jabalpur when he remarked, "Darker days are ahead and we want

---

1. Anita Inder Singh, *op, cit.*, pp. 71-72.
2. *The Leader*, 5th December, 1941.

stouter hearts and cooler minds to guide the nation destiny."[1] On reaching Bombay, Maulana Azad and Jawaharlal Nehru met Rajgopalachari at Bholabhai Desai's residence and the four Congress leaders informally discussed on 22nd December, 1941 the political situation of the country.[2]

The Congress Working Committee met at Bardoli on 23rd-30th December, 1941 under the presidentship of Maulana Azad. There was difference of opinion on the correct interpretation of the Bombay resolution. Mahatma Gandhi in a letter dated 30th December, 1941 wrote to Maulana Azad, "on re-reading the Bombay resolution I found that the differing members were right and that I had read into it a meaning which its letter could not bear. The discovery of the error makes it impossible for me to lead the Congress in the struggle for resistance to War effort on grounds in which non-violence was not indispensible. I could not, for instance, identify myself against Great Britain.[3] Jawaharlal Nehru on the other hand was of the view that in this War his sympathies were with Britian, America, Russia and China though he could not help in the War until the Congress demand for India's independence was conceded by Britain.[4] Maulana Azad, however, publicly stated that "the issue before the Congress is not violence versus non-violence but in the British Government's attitude towards the Indian demand. If Britain changes her attitude and makes an offer, the Congress would consider it. As far as non-violence is concerned, the Congress had made it clear last year in the Wardha Statement that it could not accept non-violence for the purpose of meeting external aggression. That position still stood."[5] Thereafter the Congress Working Committee passed a resolution which *interalia* stated that "only a free and independent India can be in a position to undertake the defence of the country on a national basis and be of help in

---

1. *The Leader*, 19th December, 1941.
2. Iyer, *op. cit.*, p. 131.
3. Zaidi, *op cit.*, XII. p. 449.
4. *The Leader*, 27th December, 1941.
5. *The Leader*, 24th December, 1941.

furtherance of larger causes that are emerging from the storm of the War."[1] Another resolution was passed relieving Mahatma Gandhi of his leadership of the Congress.[2] This came as a shock to some members of the Congress Working Committee and they threatened to resign. Rajendra Prasad, Sardar Patel and others issued a statement urging the members of the All India Congress Committee to exercise individual jugdement.

The Congress Working Committee was obliged to suspend individual *Satyagraha* and advised the country to organise itself to meet new peril of succession of Japanese air raids in Assam, Bengal and Vizagapatnam. If *Satyagraha* was continued and the Congress leaders were once again behind bars, the people would be deprived of guidance at a critical moment.[3] In order to sort out the differences, Maulana Azad summoned the All India Congress Committee at Wardha and left Calcutta despite influenza on 11th January, 1942 for the AICC which met at Wardha on 15th-16th, January, 1942. Commencing the proceedings, Maulana Azad explained how the Working Committee by a majority differed from Mahatma Gandhi leading to the latter's decision to be relieved of the official leadership of the Congress. He pointed out that Mahatma Gandhi was opposed to participation in the War not only on political ground but also on the ground of non-violence whereas majority of the Working Committee was opposed to it on political grounds only.[4] Maulana Azad said, "Mahatma Gandhi had a mission in life, not only for India but for the whole world. He had declared that he would not have the independence of India secured under the shadow of War and on condition that the country should support War. That is not the position with me and others and, I am prepared to accept the independence of my country at any moment it is available whether it is

---

1. *The Leader*, 31st December, 1941.
2. Zaidi, *op. cit.*, XII, p. 448.
3. *India*, pp. 555-56.
4. Zaidi, *op. cit.*, XII, p. 567.

during war or peace. My whole and only object is the attainment of the freedom of Hindustan. It does not matter if it is attained under the shadow War. The only thing is that it should be real independence."[1] Thereafter Mahatma Gandhi pleaded for the approval and confirmation of the Working Committee resolution despite his differences. He did not wish the All India Congress Committee to divide on the issue of non-violence,[2] Thus the crisis that confronted the Congress blew over and Maulana Azad returned to Calcutta.

In a letter dated 22nd January, 1942 Maulana Azad intimated Jawaharlal Nehru that he would reach Allahabad on the morning of 2nd or 3rd February, 1942 and stated, "if you think it to be advisible, you may call a meeting of those members and workers of the Provincial Committee whose presence you deem necessary on the 3rd or the 4th February in Allahabad." (42) Addressing a public meeting at Allahabad on 3rd February, 1942 he spoke mainly on the constructive programme which had been amended to suit the changed conditions. He referred to the question of co-operation in the War and said that at first the Congress wanted to bring about conditions which would enable people to live with honour but that the door was closed by the British Parliament."[3]

The British Government, however, continued to be adamant. L.S. Amery, Secretary of State for India, observed at Leeds on 4th February, 1942, "It is only Indians themselves who can give India freedom. In the absence of an agreement we can no more impose a constitution on India.... We are pledged to help India to attain, as soon as possible, after the War to the same position of freedom and equality with ourselves as is enjoyed by the Dominions."[4]

The offer of the Dominion Status was made when a succession of lightening Japanese strikes in South East Asia had left the world dizzy and Allied forces reeling on every front.

---

1. *The Leader*, 16th January, 1942.
2. Zaidi,*op. cit.*, XII, p. 567.
3. *The Leader*, 4 February, 1942.
4. *The Leader*, 6 February, 1942.

The Chinese Government was informed by its intelligence service of the statement from Tokyo that the War must be extended to India.[1] It was about this time that Generalist Chiang Kai Sheik arrived in Delhi on 9th February, 1942 in order to discuss the War situation not only with the Vicerory and the Commander-in-Chief but also with the Congress leaders. He met Maulana Azad and Jawaharlal Nehru on 11th February, 1942 and observed that if the British Government offered self government in the Dominion Status, the Congress should not reject it. Maulana Azad responded by saying, "if during the War the British Government offered Dominion Status and agreed that Indian representatives could work with a sense of freedom and responsibility, the Congress would not refuse the offer.[2] Before he left Chiang Kai Sheik made a fervent appeal demanding national government for India but he obviously failed to convince the British Government. Soon after the departure of Chiang Sheik, the Viceroy announced to celebrate China Day on 7th March, 1942. The Calcutta Radio approached Maulana Azad for recording his message to be broadcast on that day. They also informed him that Jawaharlal Nehru had already given them a message in this connection. Maulana Azad was naturally upset and on 23rd February, 1942 wrote to Jawaharlal Nehru, "Our sympathy with China needs no further elucidation but would it be a proper way of expression to participate in the function fixed by the Viceroy for their own War purpose. I do not think it to be so. I, therefore, could not give a message." (43)

When the unconquerable island of Singapore was subjugated by the Japanese on 15th February, 1942 Col. Hunt surrendered his force of sixty thousand Indian troops. This garrison of prisoners of War later become the backbone of Subhas Chandra Bose's Indian National Army. As the threat of Japanese invasion become imminent, Maulana Azad concentrated on the constructive work. In order to ensure full participa-

1. Ram Manohar Lohia, *The Mistry of Sir Stafford Cripps Mission*, Bombay, 1943.
2. *The Leader*, 18th February, 1942.

tion of women of India in the work of national reconstruction, Maulana Azad proposed formation of an advisory of Committee to the Women's Branch of the AICC comprising five members, *viz*; Mrs. Vijaya Lakshmi Pandit, Miss Mridula Sarabhai, Mrs. Aruna Asaf Ali, Mrs. Iftikharud Din with Mrs. Sucheta Kripalani as Secretary. In his letter of 2nd March, 1942 he asked Jawaharlal Nehru to suggest other names. (44)

As a result of Japanese invasion of Burma early in March, 1942 and rapid occupation of the country, the menace of War was soon at Bengal's door-steps. The panic retreat of the British forces to India had shown that the colonial apparatus had been ill-prepared for the defence of the country. The view of imminent Japanese attack, Maulana Azad started organising bands of volunteers. The Scheme he had in view was that as soon as Japanese army reached Bengal and the British army withdraw towards Bihar. the Congress should step in and capture power in the interragnum before the Japanese could establish themselves.[1] It was because of this preoccupation that Maulana Azad could not leave Calcutta. Writing Jawaharlal Nehru on 8th March, 1942 he started, "I thought that I might go to Wardha for two or three days but the delicate situation of Bengal kept me back and some intricate questions in connection with civil protection could not be left behind unsolved.…Four or five days ago a statement of Subhas Babu was broadcast from Berlin and the next day it was annuonced that it might be heard in his own voice which has been recorded. I heard it. It was the voice of Subhas Babu."(47)

In the meanwhile the Allied armies suffered serious reverses in several theatres of War. The Indian problem was troubling the progressive minds in the U.S.A., and Britain. The fall of Rangoon on 21st February, 1942 spurred the India office to pressurise whitehall for political change in India. All these factors stimulated the British Government into a realisa-

1. Azad, *op. cit.*, p. 74.

tion that some thing should be done to resolve the political deadlock in India.

In the beginning of March 1942 the Reuter's Agency informed Maulana Azad that Churchill was going to make a statement about India shortly. He, therefore, issued a circular to all the members of the Congress Working Committee on 3rd March, 1942 stating, "we do not know what would be the nature of the statement. Whatever it may be, you would agree with me that considering the delicacy of the situation it is advisible to avoid expressing any opinion individually and to wait for the meeting of the Congress Working Committee". (45)

The danger of an imminent Japanese attack on India made quite a few Congress leaders dizzy. Some of them gave vent to their feelings. When C. Vijayaraghavachariar wrote Maulana Azad in this regard, the latter raplied on 6th March, 1942, "we had not demanded power because it was a good occasion to exploit the difficulties of the British Government. We were convinced that the existing outworn system of the Indian Government was quite unfit to save the country from such a danger. The march of events has clearly demonstrated the truth of our conviction to the world. We do not want change of masters. Whether the new masters be more bad or less we have no alternative but to refuse to submit and die with the satisfaction that we are dying like honourable men". (46)

On 11th March, 1942 Churchill announced in the House of Commons the despatch of Sir Stafford Cripps, Labour Member of War Cabinet, on a mission to India. Before the arrival of Cripps, the Viceroy sent invitations to the leaders of the principal political parties. On 19th March, 1942 Maulana Azad sent an express telegram to the Private Secretary to Viceroy stating, "If Sir Stafford Cripps desires preliminary interchange of views, I shall gladly meet him. My Committee do not consider it necessary to suggest additional names." (49) Cripps arrived in Delhi on 23rd March, 1942 to negotiate with Indian leaders and released the Draft Declaration. He seems to have invited a number of Congress leaders. On 27th March, 1942 Maulana Azad sent express telegrams to

B.G. Kher, Ravishankar Shukla, Biswanathdas, Sri Krishna Sinha asking them to inform Cripps that the President was conducting talks on behalf of the Congress as desired by the Working Committee. (50)

The Draft Declaration announced by Cripps envisaged granting of Dominion Status to India leaving the dominion free to remain in or to secede from the Commonwealth. Elections to provincial legislatures would be held after the War. The Lower Houses would then act as a single electoral college and elect the constitution-making body by proportional representation. The constitution thus framed would be accepted by the British subject to the right of any province, that was unwilling, to accept the new constitution to secede from the Union. The British government would be prepared to agree to a new constitution framed by the seceding provinces.[1]

The first meeting between Maulana Azad and Cripps took place on 29th March, 1942 and a copy of the statement embodying his proposals was handed over to Maulana Azad. In order to discuss the Draft Declaration, Maulana Azad called at Delhi the Congress Working Committee which met from 29th March to 11th April, 1942. After three days careful and detailed consideration of the Draft Declaration the Congress Working Committee passed a resolution pointing out a number of vital defects and expressing their inability to recommend it to the country for acceptance.[2]

This was followed by a series of interviews and lengthy correspondence between Maulana Azad and Cripps in which the implications of the Draft Declaration were thrashed out. Maulana Azad wrote to Cripps on 1st April, 1942, "If you so desire I shell gladly meet the Commander-in-Chief...My Committee have already arrived at a decision in regard to the proposals communicated by you to us. It was my intention to send this to you this evening or possibly to take it over in person in case you wished to discuss any point contained init. This

1. Nicholas Mansergh (ed). *The Transfer of Power* I, (London, 1970), pp. 82-84.
2. Zaidi, *op. cit.*, XII, p. 572-74.

decision naturally covers other points also apart from defence." (51) The emphasis on defence led Cripps to reconsider the matter and he wrote to Maulana Azad on 7th Appril, 1942 suggesting a formula for Defence. (52) Maulana Azad again met Cripps on 9th April, 1942 and an agreement seemed to be in sight in the presence of Colonel Johnson, President Roosevelt's personal representative, who had come to New Delhi to discuss military problems. A compromise formula had been worked out by which an Indian would be in charge of the Defence Department while the British Commander-in-Chief would retain control over field operations and head a War Department whose functions were specified. In the meanwhile the Viceroy, Linlithgow, and Commander-in-Chief, Wavel, were seriously worried that Cripps was conceding too much real power to the Congress and in concert with Churchill they succeeded in blocking the settlement at the last moment. The War Cabinet in its cable of 9th April, 1942 sharply pulled up Cripps for not adequately consulting the Viceroy and the Commander-in-Chief as also for giving Johnson too much scope. It further deplored allusion to a National Government and emphasized the need to bring the whole matter back to Cabinet Plan which he went out to urge.[1]

Maulana Azad wrote to Cripps on 10th April, 1942, "Defenee, at any time, and more particularly in War time, is of essential importance and without it a National Government functions in a very limited field. Apart from this consideration it was obvious that the whole purpose of your proposals and our talks centred round the urgency of the problems created by the threat of the invasion of India...Popular resistance must have a national background and both the soldier and the civilian must feel that they are fighting for their country's freedom under national leadership."(52) Cripps sent a reply to Maulana Azad's letter in which he stated that he could not accept the points raised by the Congress with regard to defence and national government. In his letter of

---

1. Mansergh, *op. cit.*, I, pp. 707-708.

11th April, 1942 to Cripps Maulana Azad stated, "It seems that there has been a progressive deterioration in the British Government's attitude as our negotiations proceeded. What we were told in our first talk with you is now denied or explained away. You told me that there would be a national government which would function as a Cabinet and that the position of the Viceroy would be analogous to that of the king in England vis a vis his Cabinet." (53) There is yet another axplanation as to why Cripps Mission had failed. With the progress of his conversation Cripps is said to have felt 'the deadening influence of non-violence upon Congress leaders and their desire under certain conditions, to make peace with Japan."[1] It is true that the All Congress leaders like Sardar Patel felt convinced that the Allies were going to loose the War.[2] Mahatma Gandhi described the Cripps offer as a "post dated cheque on a tottering bank"[3], but as far as the Cripps offer was concerned Mahatma Gandhi had given full freedom to the members of the Congress Working Committee. Talking about the failure of Cripps Mission at a press conference on 11th April, 1942 Maulana Azad said "I, however, regret to say that first impression of the picture created as a result of my earlier interview with Sir Stafford gradually became blurrd as the discussion on material point proceeded from stage to stage and when I last met him on the night of April, 9, the whole picture had completely faded out. I think I must clarify the position created by certain speculation in a section of the press as regards Mahatma Gandhi's part in the discussions. In fact Mahatma Gandhi made it clear to the Working Committee that they were perfectly free to come to their own decisions on the merits of the proposals. (79)

Failing in his attempt to solve the Indian political problems, Cripps in the course of an interview at Karachi said that Congress leaders first went to Col. Johnson who

---

1. Lohia, *op. cit.*, pp. 4-5.
2. Munshi, *op. cit.*, p. 75.
3. H.M. Searvai, *Partition of India*, (Bombay, 1989), p. 24.

acted as a meditator in his personal capacity. This charge was vehemently refuted by Jawaharlal Nehru and Maulana Azad, the Congress negotiators with Cripps. In a statement to the press Jawaharlal Nehru clarified that Col. Johnson did not interfere in any way though of course he expressed his desire that a satisfactory settlement should be reached.[1] Similarly Maulana Azad in a press statement said, "On or about April, 1, a common friend informed Pandit Jawaharlal Nehru that Col. L. Johnson was anxious to meet him and would be glad if a meeting could be arranged at his residence. Accordingly Pandit Nehru met him. Again it was by a pure accident that on April 3, while I was on my way to a meeting of Working Committee, I went to Pandit Nehru's residence, which was on my way, to pick him up and there I found Col. Johnson. Naturally we met and had a brief talk. At the end of this talk, Col. Johnson expressed a desire that in the event of the Working Committee coming to an adverse decision he should be allowed a chance to see if he could be helpful before the Committee's final verdict was formally communicated to Sir Stafford Cripps. His wish was so obviously in the interest of the common object...that I saw no objection in complying with it...I must make it perfectly clear that no body on behalf of the Congress sought either Col. Johnson's or President Roosevelt's intervention, although in the very nature of things Col. Jonson's friendly interest was appreciated." (80)

The failure of the Cripps Mission created mixed feelings in the minds of some of the members of the Congress Working Committee. Believing that an end to the Congress-League differences was the necessary precursor to any constitutional settlement, C. Rajagopalachari pushed through the Congress Legislative Party in Madras two resolutions. One urging resumation of ministerial responsibilities in provinces and the other favouring settlement with the Muslim League on the basis of the latter's demand for separation[2] Since both these

1. *The Indian Annual Register* I, January-June, 1942, p. 242.
2. Zaidi, *op. cit.*, XII, p. 584.

resolutions were at variance with the declared policy of the Congress, Maulana Azad issued a statement to the press at Calcutta on 25th April, 1942 and said, "It greatly astonished and pained me that a man like Mr. Rajagopalachari, inspite of his being a member of the Congress Working Committee, should have adopted such an attitude. I would assure you that any personal relationship, howsoever dear to me, can not deter me for a moment from discharging my duty as a President of the Congress." (81) Consequently on 30th April, 1942 Rajagopalachari submitted his resignation from the Congress Working Committee and stated, "I believe that I should be failing in my duty if I do not endeavour to get people to think and act in the direction which my conviction leads to."[1]

In order to review the political situation in the light of the rejection of the Cripps proposals, Maulana Azad called the AICC which met at Allahabad on 29th May-2nd June, 1942.[2] Commencing the precedings, Maulana Azad pointed out, "The picture gradually disappeared from our sight and Sir Stafford finally gave such a different shape to the picture that we could by no stretch of imagination even care to look at it. Defence is of primary importance at this moment. It is defence that matters most when we have drawn so close to the War."[3]

A new situation arose when the Japanese forces occupied Burma and advanced towards Assam. The AICC at its meeting held on 29th April-2nd May 1942 noted with indignation the arrangement made for and the treatment accorded to evacuees and refugees from Malaya and Burma to India. Such arrangements for evacuation as were made were meant principally for the European population and at every step racial discrimination was in evidence.[4] The AICC, therefore, decided to send a Medical Unit under Dr. B. C. Roy for the relief of evacuees coming from Burma.[5] On 28th April, 1942

---

1. Zaidi, *op. cit.*, XII, pp. 465-66.
2. *Ibid.*, pp. 384-85.
3. *The Leader*, 30th April, 1942.
4. Zaidi, *op. cit.*, XII, pp. 384-85.
5. *The Indian Annual Register*, 1942, p. 302.

Maulana Azad sent a telegram from Allahabad to Dr. B.C. Roy stating, "please take immediate steps. Organise Unit in co-operation relief societes. Wire estimate expenditure and likely date departure Unit." (54) Simultaneously Maulana Azad issued an appeal stating, "The sending of this Unit will cost a considerable sum of money but the object is such that I am sure sufficient funds will be forthcoming." (55, 83)

In case of Japanese attack on Bengal, the British Government had decided to follow the scorched earth policy and had prepared a plan to blow up important bridges and to destroy factories and industrial installations. There was great anxiety and urest in the area.[1] Under these circumstances, Maulana Azad was compelled to postpone his visit to Bombay in order to meet Mahatma Gandhi. On 13th May, 1942 he wrote to Jawaharlal Nehru, "the affairs of Bengal have stuck to me in such a way that I had to postpone my visit. The Chittagong air attack has created a feeling here that Calcutta will also be attacked within a few days. Moreover new and difficult problems have suddenly arisen in connection with the coastal population of Bengal." (57)

Maulana Azad could not leave Calcutta as he was busy during May-June, 1942 gearing up the Congress organisation, in building up public resistance against the anticipated Japanese attack on Calcutta.[2] On 31st May, 1942 he wrote to Jawaharlal Nehru, "the refugees from Burma are pouring in Sylhet and Karimganj. Most of them succumb to epidemic disease. The local Congress Committee had made arrangements for doctors. They were in need of medicines, elothes and male nurses which we have supplied them. Owing to the air-raid by Japan on the borders of Assam, a new situation has arisen in the whole province. People leave the cities for villages. Marwari grain dealers have totally vacated the province which has caused great dislocation of grain business." (62)

The Japanese attacks threatened not only the freedom but the very existence of India. In order to take stock of the

1. Maulana Azad, *op. cit.*, p. 73.
2. *Ibid.*, p. 74.

political situation the Congress Working Committee met at Wardha on 14th July, 1942 and was presided over by Maulana Azad. There was difference of opinion among the members of the Congress Working Committee as to the line of action to be adopted for resisting the Japanese invasion. Rajendra Prasad, Sardar Patel, Acharya J.B. Kriplani and other members of the Congress Working Committee were supporting Mahatma Gandhi's non-violent *Satyagraha* but Maulana Azad and Jawaharlal Nehru had a strong conviction that it was not proper to start a non-violent movement at such a juncture. The Congress Working Committee, however, accepted Mahatma Gandhi's point of view and passed a resolution on 14th July 1942 which *interalia* stated, "if such withdrawal takes place with good-will it would result in establishing a stable Provisional Government in India and co-opration between this Government and the United Nations in resisting agression and helping China."[1]

In order to discuss the decision of the Congress Working Committee a meeting of the AICC was held on 7th-8th, August 1942 in spacious and beautifully decorated pandal in the Gowalia Tank Maidan, Bombay. This session, presided over by Maulana Azad, passed the famous 'Quit India' resolution which endorsed the Congress Working Committee resolution and stated that "events subsequent to it have given it further justification and have made it clear that immediate ending of British rule in India is an urgent necessity both for the sake of India and for success of the cause of the United Nations.[2] Speaking from the chair, Maulana Azad clarified that 'Quit India' demand did not mean the physical removal of all the Britishers from India but only meant transfer of power to the Indian hands. He made it abundantly clear, "if the Muslim League is willing to negotiate, he would persuade the Congress within twenty four hours to start negotiations." (84) He referred to the offer made by him to the Muslim League to solve the communal problem. The offer in fact was

1. Zaidi, *op. cit.*, XII, p. 471.
2. *Ibid.*, pp. 390-91.

that "provided the Muslim League co-operated fully with the Congress demand for immediate independence without the slightest reservation, subject of course to the proviso that independent India will permit the operations of the Allied armies in order to check Axis aggression and thus to help both China and Russia, the Congress will have no objection to the British Government transferring all the powers it to day exercises to the Muslim League on behalf of the whole of India, including the so-called Indian India and the Congress will not only not obstruct any government that the Muslim League may form on behalf of the people but will even join the government in running the machinery of the free state."[1]

Concluding his speech Maulana Azad said that he was addressing a letter to President Roosevelt and approaching the Viceroy for an honourable settlement.[2] On the same day he issued a statement to the press wherein he said, "In the present world conflagration India could side with only one set of combatants. But for India to effectively participate with the right side in this War it was necessary to properly mobilise the people of India...However much one wished, it would not be possible to rouse Indians to enthusiastic participation in this War till the right thing was done by India, namely, the country was made free." (85)

The British Government reacted to the 'Quit India' resolution by arresting the Congress leaders on the morning of 9th August, 1942 in the expectation that the arrests would finish off any contemplated movement.[3] Maulana Azad, Jawaharlal Nehru, Sarojini Naidu and Sardar Patel were sent to Ahmadnagar Fort jail. The leaderless and unorganised supporters of the Congress rose in revolt in various parts of the country. By the end of the month Linlithgow wrote to Churchill, "I am engaged here in meeting by far the most serious rebellion since that of 1857, the gravity and extent of

1. Sitaramaya, *op. cit.*, p. 350.
2. Iyer, *op. cit.*, p. 159.
3. Anita Inder Singh, *op. cit.*, p. 85.

which we have so far concealed from the world for reason of military security.[1]

In sum, then, Maulana Abul Kalam Azad belonged to that small company of statesmen who were also men of letters. Endowed with the temper of a philosopher, he was averse to the storms and stresses of politics and repeatedly refused political offices but the tumultous times he lived in dragged him out from the cloister of a recluse into the battleground of politics. His dexterous and alert mind was at its best at the negotiating-table, making his point with scholarly details. He had a penchant for reconciling various and sometimes conflicting points of view and his clear and farsighted vision made him a statesman extra-ordinary. He contributed the vital intellectual dimension to India's strugge for freedom and was indeed one of the theoriticians of the Indian National Congress.

1. Mansergh, *op. cit.*, I, p. 43.

PART 1

Letters and Telegrams

(1)

To Motilal Nehru[1] Circular Letter[2] 1st November, 1923[3]

It is more than 5 weeks since the conclusion of the Delhi Congress[4] and the swift passage of time will soon bring us to the last week of the year when the Congress reassembles at Cocanada.[5] None can deny the fact that we attained a considerable measure of success in terminating the domestic squabbles of the Congress and paying the way for fruitful efforts in new direction but the preliminary steps taken in grappling with a more formidable evil, namely, the recent accentuation of communal differences and the embitterment of intercommunal relations, did not go beyond arresting its rapid progress. Signs of recrudescence of the progressive tendencies of the said evil so far from being wholly wanting lay upon us the imperative duty of immediately resuming our adjourned deliberations and devoting effectual endeavours to the final solution of the questions connected therewith. An informal conference of prominent leaders of thought appears to me to be the need of the hour not merely for this object but also for considering the programme of work we have to place before the country for the ensuing year to ensure the concentration of the country's energy on a vigorous renewal of our struggle for freedom. I take the liberty of supposing that you will endorse the view that the Congress in the present condition of its organisation seems almost unequal to the task of taking any definitive steps; the existing Congress Committees being almost without any motive-power behind or a really practical programme of work before them. Virutally, the Congress Committees seem to have ceased to function. Such activity as is obsevrable is centred on the electioneering campaign for the Councils, and is, therefore, necessarily confined to a section of Congressmen. This is a state of affairs, which in my humble opinion, calls for an informal conference of leading Congressmen for devoting their earnest thoughts to the questions of the hour with a view to evolve a mature and effectual programme of work to be placed before the Cocanada Congress. I have consulted Hakim Ajmal Khan, Pandit Madan

Mohan Malviya, Lala Lajpat Rai, Pandit Motilal Nahru, Mrs. Sarojni Naidu, Dr. Ansari and some other friends, all of whom have endorsed my view. The informal conference has accordingly been fixed for the 30th November 1923 at Delhi, and I earnestly hope that recognising the eminently urgent nature of the object for which the conference is being convened, you will not fail to allot it the first place in your engagements and will contribute your indispensable quota to its deliberations. Kindly intimate your arrival to Mr. M. Asaf Ali,[8] the Secretary Provincial Congress Committee, Delhi.

A.K. Azad

(2)

To[1] Seshadri Srinivasa Iyengar[2] Telegram[3] 25th June, 1927

In my opinion sitting will be best at Calcutta.

Abul Kalam

(3)

To[1] Motilal Nehru Telegram[2] 4th May, 1929

You can add my name to signatories.[3]

Abul Kalam

(4)

To[1] Jawaharlal Nehru,[2] Telegram[3] 23rd September 1933

Reaching Monday mail wire if you are Lucknow.

Abul Kalam

(5)

To[1] Jawaharlal Nehru Telegram[2] 25th September 1933

Got no seat owing Puja rush Now reaching Wardha when you there.

Abul Kalam

(6)

To[1] C. Vijiaraghavachariar[2] Letter[3] 27th May, 1937

If I say I am thankful to have received your kind letter, believe me it would hardly suffice to express my true feelings. I have felt something more than merely be thankful. What could be the subject of more happiness to me than to find such appreciative high opinions of my humble services expressed by so venerable a person like you, who has contributed such life-long services to the country, and all the more, I am endowed with the blessings of his prayers!

Even to this day, I have not forgotten the very time when on the occasion of the Allahabad Unity Conference[4] I had requested you to stay a few days more. You had conceded to my request and tears began rolling down from your eyes uncontrollably! The sight of those tears has left such a deep impression upon my heart that often it so happened that their recollection made my own eyes filled up with tears.

Our destination is still far and the way is beset with wearisome obstacles. Nevertheless, we much have to keep marching on. We are not to see whether we have gained the destination but to continue on the journey in quest unfailingly. The saying of a Persian poet is always on my lips :

"The pilgrim of Love can never face failure,
Because the very keeping on the pilgrimage is in itself the greatest success!".

Hoping you will always remember me in your prayers. With kind regards.

A.K. Azad

(7)

To[1] Ranjit Pandit[2] Telegram[3] 6th September, 1938

Your telegram just received. Telephone number 26 if necessary.

Abul Kalam

(8)

To[1] Rajendra Prasad Telegram[2] 14th September, 1938

Bardoloi telephoned me after giving undertaking for coalition Ministry.[3] Starting Shellong to-day, shall inform you later.

Abul Kalam Azad

(9)

To[1] Rajendra Prasad Telegram[2] 29th October, 1938

Owing indisposition journey postponed. Please decide Bhagalpore Gaya affairs[3] removing Muslim complaints which have perturbed Muslim nationalists. Immediate remedy necessary. Please telephone me to-night

Abul Kalam Azad

(10)

To[1] Nilakantha Das,[2] Godavarish Misra[3] and Chintamani Misra[4] Letter[5] 27th December, 1938

Babu Rajendra Prasad was to go to Cuttack in connection with the Orissa Tenancy Amendment Bill. It was decided that he will also go through the complaints against the Hon'ble B.N. Das, Premier, Orissa. It is a pity that he is not keeping good health and is still unable to undertake the journey. As this is a matter which can no more be delayed, I wish to expedite it. But as it is difficult for me also to go to Cuttack at present, I think it would be better if you take the trouble of coming to Calcutta on the 1st January, 1939. The Premier will also come and the needful will be done here. Kindly let me know by wire that you are coming here on the 1st January so that I may inform the Premier also; or you may inform him directly so that he may start on 31st instant for Calcutta.

Abul Kalam Azad

(11)

To[1] N. Kanungo[2] Letter 28th December, 1938

I am in receipt of your letter of 27th December, 1938. I have sent letters to the three gentlemen, according to the proposal of Mr. Bishwanath Das and am waiting for their replies. On receipt of replies about their arrival here on the first January, I shall inform you by wire so that Mr. Das may also come here.[3] In case I do not get any reply (and) they (cannot) come here on the first, I shall inform you about it even then.

Abul Kalam Azad

(12)

To[1] Jawaharlal Nehru Letter[2] 17th April, 1939

When I think of my accident at Allahabad[3] I find that nothing more could have been done for my comfort and treatment by my own people here had it happened in Calcutta. Indeed the nearest and dearest of my relatives could not have left more than you did for me there. I do not know how to express my feelings of gratitude to you. Believe me my heart is extremely grateful for your love and kindness.

There are numerous ordinary things which tend to create deep feelings of heart. While coming from Allahabad you looked into the very minor details about my comforts for a journey which had to last for only a night. I did not know how many things have been sent with me. Reaching here I found that even a bottle of Eue de Cologne was placed in the basket.

I do not know whether you have seen the letters of Subhas[4] to Gandhiji.[5] It is a pity that Subhas babu is exactly in the position where he was before Tripuri,[6] and there is no hope that he will improve the situation by acting on the Tripuri resolution. On the one hand he calls the Pant resolution[7] against the constitution and *ultra vires*, on the other he wants Gandhiji to accept certain conditions. Alongwith this he does not hesitate in making the extravagent assertion that the Pant resolution would have been lost, had the Socialist group[8] not become neutral.

However thers is no hope of the Congress moving along Subhas babu. The whole thing will come to dead stop. We have, therefore, to chalk out the further line of action.

I consider the affair of Subhas babu to be neither a struggle between the right and the left, nor the question of composite and homogeneous Working Committee. It is only a matter of Subhas and some of his supporters. It matters little in what form the tangle comes to an end, we have to consider these questions independently and specifically, in order to reach a solution.

I hope you have received my last letter and you have phoned to Lucknow about Sultan Ahmad.[9]

A.K. Azad

(13)

To[1] Jawaharlal Nehru Letter[2] 5th July, 1939

I expected to meet you in Bombay but owing to the slow progress of recovery I could not undertake the journey. Dr. Roy[3] thinks that it will take at least one month more to become normal.

I am writing this letter for a special matter. Chammanlal[4], who was sometime a reporter of the *Hindustan Times*, will meet you. Why do you not take him on the staff of the *National Herald*? He has acquired sufficient experience in Jounralism, and I think the *National Herald* stands much in need of such men.

He is known to me for the last fifteen years. There are a few defects in him but I do not think that they will hinder the work.

Much had to be discussed with you about the present and the future but after you return from Ceylon[5] we may get a chance of meeting each other.

Please convey my message of love to Indra[6] when you write to her next.

A.K. Azad

(14)

To[1] Rajendra Prasad Letter[2] 10th July, 1939

Your letter of the 3rd instant to hand. The Punjab affairs need our immediate attention but you are right in saying that they cannot be settled unless a strong man goes there. So far as I am concerned, I am yet unable to use my leg. In the opinion of Bidhan Roy, it still requires one month's treatment which means that I shall be able to walk about by the middle of August. If someone has to go there immediately, I think either you yourself, Sardar Patel or Pandit Jawaharlal should go. Jawaharlal is going to Ceylon and he will not be able to return before August. Now the matter devolves on you or Patel. No one else can be of any use there.

The malady of the Punjab is chronic and deep-seated. It will not be sufficient to glean at the surface only. The real causes of the disease are to be diagnosed and firm steps are to be taken to root out the disease absolutely. If none of you or Mr. Patel can give time for it, then nothing can be done but to wait for my recovery.

The attitude of Subhas Babu as well as of the P.C.C. Bengal (has) created an important problem. It is necessary that the verdict (is given) unhesitatingly and without any weakness.[3]

A.K. Azad

(15)

To[1] Jawaharlal Nehru Letter[2] 17th August, 1939

Thanks for your letter. I have already sent to you two letters one after the other on your Allahabad address. I hope they have reached you.

I do not know whether Rajendra Babu[3] had presented my letter before the Committee or not.[4] He himself and Vallabhbhai[5] had insisted to send my opinion—in case I would not attend—and therefore I had written my opinion in detail. In my opinion the attitude of Subhas Babu was wrong and it was necessary for the Working Committee to express its opinion. But I had suggested not to show too much strictness at this occasion. I proposed that the Working Committee should pass a resolution on the lines of the one passed by you in U.P., and leave the rest to the President.[6] The President may then correspond with them and if they agree with the resolution of the Committee, then they may simply be removed from their present office. But there should be no bar to their next year's election.

I had given you the trouble to talk over the phone as I thought that you would take part in the consideration of this matter. But now it transpires that you remained practically aloof, and the decision was made in the absence of your agreement.[7]

A.K. Azad

(16)

To[1] Rajendra Prasad Telegram[2] 27th August, 1939

Staying here at present Stop Patna suitable. Wire

Abul Kalam Azad

(17)

To[1] Rajendra Prasad Telegram[2] 3rd September 1939

Reaching Calcutta tomorrow morning Meeting should be called without delay[3] Wire Calcutta.

Abul Kalam Azad

(18)

To[1] Rajendra Prasad Telegram[2] 5th September 1939

Better fix Working Commmittee tenth.[3] Indefiniteness must be ended. My presence Lucknow unavoidable eight ninth if health permits. Why not fix Lucknow or Allahabad. Please wire express.

Abul Kalam Azad

(19)

To[1] Jawaharlal Nehru Letter[2] 11th November, 1939

The Hindustani Committee[3] Patna has been further postpond to December 15 instead of 18th November. Now I can reach Allahabad on the 19th without any hitch. I shall reach there by the Punjab Mail and probably Bidhan[4] will be also with me.

My fears about Assam have come to be true. There are only two Congressmen out of the eight Ministers. The remaining six are non-Congressites and naturally they are averse to leave the Ministry. In the words of Bordoloi,[5] "Congress circles themselves and some Congress office-holders too, are supporting them".

However Bordoloi assures me that he would resign till the 12th November. It is hoped that (he) may be able to do so.

I wish to remind you (about) an important matter. Fazlul Haq had said, in reply to your statement, that he would inform you on reaching Calcutta. More than a week has already passed. Please wire to him immediately that you are waiting for his information so that you may be able to chalk out your programme accordingly. A copy of this telegram should also be given to the Press.

Your reply has absolutely upset Fazlul Haq. All his colleagues are blaming him for his folly. This is the most opportune time to bring him to his senses by persistently forcing the issues at him so that the absurdity may end for all time to come and the public should not get a chance of forgetting this episode.

A.K. Azad

(20)

To[1] Rajendra Prasad Letter[2] 28th November, 1939

Sarat Babu has sent me yesterday a cheque of Rs. 5,000 and a fixed deposit receipt for Rs.10,075 in connection with the Assembly Party Fund. Now a balance of Rs. 521/13/6 remains in his current account which he has not transferred in order that "the Account may remain open in the Bank for future". As nothing was said in the resolution of the Working Committee for the future he thinks that he will continue depositing the contributions of the members in the Bank as usual. I did not deem it expedient to say anything to him in this connection at present. We shall think over it in future.

He has sent a lengthy letter to me about this matter which he has requested me to present to the next Working Committee. He has taken strong exception to the decision of the Working Committee.[3] I have acknowledged his letter saying that I will present it before the next Working Committee.

I hope you are doing well. I am still as before yet I have decided to start for Patna on December 4. There we shall have the occasion to meet and talk in detail.

A.K. Azad

(21)

To[1] Rajendra Prasad Letter[2] 3rd January, 1940

I am fully in agreement with your opinion which you have formed about Utkal.[3] We have decided to take a final step about Bengal, if the Provincial Committee to be held on the 6th allows the decision of the Executive to stand as it is. The

Working Committee should be called for this, not on the 15th, but earlier. You have written to the Bengal Provincial (Committee) to send its statement to you till the 10th January. You can call the Working Committee on the 11th by telegram.[4] I write this simply because I want to get a chance of going sooner to the Punjab.[5]

A.K. Azad

(22)

To[1] Rajendra Prasad Letter[2] 5th January, 1940

Many telegrams have been received from the Punjab, saying that the Tribunal there has been formed on party lines by the P.C.C., and which is not expected to work in a non-partisan spirit. It is also said that the men selected for a Tribunal have no social standing. An ordinary clerk of the Pratap Office has been made a member.

The Tribunal would have been appointed in August last. No complaint was received at that time. The difficulty now is that the complaints are pouring in just at the time of the election. I cannot make out what to do just at present in this matter. The election of the delegates will begin there from the 8th January.

Moreover, the complaints regarding the P.C.C. should go to the office, or direct to you—not to me.

However, I am sending the telegrams to you. You may please wire them some reply.

There is a complaint from Jammu that the Punjab Congress has ignored their delegation. The telegram is enclosed herewith for inquiry and necessary action.

A.K. Azad

(23)

To[1] Rajendra Prasad Telegram[2] 27th February, 1940

Mail missed. Now starting Delhi Express with Gandhiji.[3]

Abul Kalam Azad

(24)

To[1] Sarat Chandra Bose Letter[3] 2nd March, 1940

I had received your telegram at Patna yesterday to the effect that the Bengal Congress Assembly Party requests the Parliamentary Sub-Committee to reconsider the nomination of the indirect election of the Bengal Council. In reply to which I wired you that I was reaching the next morning (March 2nd), by the Punjab Mail and asked you therein to meet me in the morning to discuss the matter in detail and consider the situation.[4] On reaching here I informed you of my arrival and was waiting to see you. But it is now 11 o'clock and you have not yet come. The election is to take place to-day at 12 noon. Under the circumstances there is no option for me but the decision, which the Parliamentary Sub-Committee had reached, should stand. I am sure that every member of the Party will abide by the decision.[5]

Abul Kalam Azad

(25)

To[1] J-B. Kripalani[2] Letter 27th March, 1940

Yours of the 15th. I had already seen your circular regarding the Congress resolution in the Press and I was happy over it. I think you did well in issuing these circulars.

Fifteenth is a suitable date for the Working Committee. Please do not change it. I want to send additional invitation(s) to the following gentlemen :

1. Pattabhi[3]
2. Dr. B.C. Roy.
3. Master Tara Singh[4]

   (Inform him that the Working Committee would like to gather from him some information about the Shromani Akali Dal).[5]

I am issuing a statement on the National Week. I hope to reach Allahabad on the 30th.

A.K. Azad

(26)

To[1] Jawaharlnl Nehru Letter[2] 17th March, 1940

When on the 15th morning you handed me on the train the English version of my Address,[3] I just skipped over it to form a general impression of the translation. I had no time until now to go through it at leisure. Now that I am comparatively free, I have made a close study of the document. The impression it has created on me compels me shake off my usual reserve for the movement and offer my sincere tribute to your first-rate intellect and your exceptional talents. Your mastery over English extends far beyond what I imagined until now. I dare say some of the most accomplished men of our day could hardly undertake to perform a task of such magnitude in so many days whereas it took you just a few hours and that too, without any special effort.

Translating, in a way, is much more difficult than composing in original. It is by no means easy to maintain the literary content of the original writing and at the same time convey through translation the literary style of the writer. Only a person with equal command over both the languages could have attempted such a task. What particularly strikes me in your translation is the fact that no feature of the original has suffered through it, and you have conveyed my Urdu literary style so successfully in English that I should not be surprised if it occurs to the reader that the original was in English and not Urdu.[4]

An qually impressive feature is your remarkable grasp of the architectonic imagination from which the details flow. You have perfectly visualized my imagination which gave form and shape to my sentences and composition. In fact, you had a full picture of my theme when you started translating. Surely, it was a stupendous task, specially when my own compositions could not directly assist you.

In some places you have slightly changed the Urdu version and expanded or abbreviated it to suit the exigencies of the English rendering. I have carefully taken note of all these variations and I am happy to find that you have improved upon my writing in some cases. In no case, has the spirit or the form of my writing suffered. Commenting on the Viceregal declaration I wrote as follows : Now, "ba-mushkil" is the keyword of my metaphorical expression. While maintaining the background of my metaphor you have conveyed it as follows :

"After reading page after page the curtain is at last lifted with hesitation and we have a glimpse. . . ."

What I wanted to convey through "ba-mushkil" your expanded phrase brings out the meaning with greater emphasis and I must confess that your version is more apt than mine. This is just to mention one among many such embellishments.

I expect to reach Allahabad probably on the 30th. I hope you will be staying in Allahabad until then.

A.K. Azad

(27)

Te[1] Jamnalal Bajaj Telegram[3] 12th April, 1940

Reaching tomorrow mail.

Azad

(28)

To[1] Jawaharlal Nehru Letter[2] 24th April 1940

Thanks for your letter of 21st April. I agree with you that if Krishna Menon[3] goes to America on his own accord, it would be useful to the demand of the time to some extent. Had it come before us previous to the meeting of the Working Committee, it would have been decided in it. However I am writing to the General Secretary to send $100/- immediately to him, and hope you would make arrangements for at least another $100/- from Bombay.

You say that I should write a letter to him also. I think that if I write to him as the President, it would necessarily mean that he is going there on behalf of the Congress; and as you yourself write, it would be against expediency to carry the matter to such an extent. It would be better if you write him a letter saying : 'I am glad to hear that you are going to America. I hope your presence there would enable them to understand the existing Indian situation." Your letter will fully help him in giving him a responsible capacity. And along with it this would save the position which might be created in writing it directly on behalf of the President.

There were three houses of friends in Mussoorie which have already been occupied. Can any one amongst your friends arrange a house at Mussoorie? If it is not possible in this way, I am ready to pay rent. The house should however be good and commodious. Please wire for the arrangement if you have any such person in mind. The weather of Calcutta is telling upon me.

I thought of Nainital and Almora after Mussoorie, I am writing to Pantji[4] about it.

A.K. Azad

(29)

To[1] Jawaharlal Mehru Letter[2] 9th May, 1940

I had received your telegram about Mussoorie for which I am obliged. Due to arrangements in Nainital, I gave up the idea of Mussoorie.

I reached here on the 6th. Circumstances permitting, I shall stay here upto July. You might stay in Bombay till the end of May and then leave for Allahabad. Why not come to Nainital and stay here with me for some time ? You can work here on the compilation of the report of the Planning Committee.[3] There would be no difference between Allahabad and Nainital, so far as the Provincial work is concerned. You can remain in touch with the work equally from here as from Allahabad. Moreover your presence here would be useful for prompt consultations about many matters.

I had a talk with Mr. A. Patwardhan[4] at Wardha.[5] He said that he would talk to me on another occasion but he could not see me. Please inquire of him about the membership of the Working Committee. I give you the trouble as I do not know his address. Socialist friends have proved to be quite hopeless. They have not courage enough to work. They fear opposition and dare not stand firmly on their own legs. I expected to get some help from them at this critical juncture,[6] but all my hopes proved to be false.

If Patwardhan is not prepared for it, some other person should be nominated soon. Could you suggest some name ?

The Imperial Tobacco Company has sent a note to me which shows the nature of the strike to be quite different from what it was represented by the workers. However, I am trying to find out some means of honourable compromise.[7]

A.K. Azad

(30)

To[1] Jawaharlal Nehru Letter[2] 25th May 1940

Thanks for your letter of the 16th instant. I read the statement of Rajendra Babu in the papers with surprise and in the meanwhile I received his letter which gave me clearly the trend of his thoughts. I am sorry that I cannot send you a copy of the letter which I sent him in reply, as it was in Urdu and no copy but of official letters is kept in the office. So far as the present attitude of the Congress is concerned, this letter was nearly the same as yours. I am pleased to find that our thoughts are going the same way in this respect and it is most gratifying to find that Gandhiji is also in full agreement with it.

The statement of Asafali[3] was still more objectionable as compared to that of Rajan Babu. In fact it grieved me. I wrote him two biting letters one after the other. Now he assures me that he will abstain from such statements in future.

Whatever you write in your letters addressed to me and Rajan Babu are quite correct so far as the Congress attitude is concerned. There seems to be no reason why any question of change should arise at this stage. But alongwith it, you have written two things to which I do not agree and I wonder how they can be adjusted in the plan which your mind is forming in relation to the Congress's line of action. You say in the letter of Rajan Babu "The *Satyagraha* is not immediately indicated even if we were ready for it. I think it would be wrong for us at this particular moment, when Britain is in peril, to take advantage of her distress and rush at her throat." You have also expressed this idea in the Lucknow speech and the *Pioneer* thought it necessary to quote your original words: "*Yeh baat Hindostan ki shaan kay Khilaaf hae, ke woh England kee Kamzoree say faa-e-daa uthaa kar iss waqt satyagraha Shuroo kar dey.*" I absolutely fail to grasp this mode of thinking. In fact this very method is totally wrong that we should first formulate such premisses in matters of political struggle and then draw wrong conclusions about our line of action. I do not know what is the "*shaan*" of India. I only want to know what is the considered decision, and where does it lead to ? We cannot grope in the dark like blind men. We should adopt a way with open eyes. Nothing can be more absurd than to chalk out a way and then refuse to tread upon it.

We gave Britain fullest opportunity to take us with her but she stubbornly refused to do so. We were forced to decide not to participate in this Imperialistic War. If our present stand is such that it "Embarasses" her (in the words of Gandhiji) or in your words it is against the "*shaan*" of India—there can be no remedy to it. We are not responsible for it, it lies with the imprudent vanity of the British Government.

You say that we should not launch *Satyagraha* at this moment. But, what do you mean by *Satyagraha* ? Would be a new declaration of war which the Congress has yet to formulate? The war of the Congress is nothing but to stop any help in the war. This checking process has not yet been carried onward from a certain limit in actual practice. It is inevitable to carry it further on in future. It would automatically take the form of Civil Disobedience because of the existence of War ordinances and individual arrests.

If your moral philosophy be taken to be correct in relation to the dignity of India, it will mean only one thing—

i.e. Ramgarh decision was absolutely against the honour and dignity of India.

You tell further on in this letter about our future attitude if some form of agreement is reached with the Government. You say, "even if all this is agreed to (i.e. Independence, Self-determination, and Constituent Assembly with adult franchise) it does not follow that we throw our main power into the War."

But if it does not follow, why should we hope that British Government would give us all that we ask for ? Surely, she can grant all these things reluctantly, if forced to do so. But there is no question of using force at this juncture, when even the use of moral force of *Satyagraha* seems to be against the "dignity" of India.

I do not understand how this confused and illogical conception could find a way to your mind. You, least of all, are not expected to think in such a way.

I hope your stay in Lahore will be fully helpful to its activities.

I have received a telegram of Sikander Hayat today, a copy of which has probably been sent to you also. I have wired in reply that the responsibility of the present situation lies not on us but on the British Government.

A.K. Azad

(31)

To[1] J.B. Kripalani Letter[2] 2nd June, 1940

It is hoped that the invitations to the members of the Working Committee for the 17th June might have been duly sent by now. Following persons may also be invited at (on) this occassion :

1. Acharya Narendra Deo.[3]
2. Achyut Patwardhan,
3. Dr. Pattabhi Sitaramayyah,[4]
4. Mrs. Vijay Lakshmi Pundit.[5]

A.K. Azad

(32)

To[1] Jawaharlal Nehru Letter[2] 19th July, 1940

Thanks for your letter of 18th instant[3]. Please re-read my statement[4]. I did not say that the resolution[5] was unanimously passed. I have only explained the mental aspect of the resolution, saying that all were clear in their "minds" that in case the Indian demand is accepted, she (India) should participate in (the) war. Accordingly the *Statesman* and others have taken the same meaning of the statement.

I shall be obliged if you do not issue any statement about it just at present till we meet in Poona. I wish to have a detailed talk with you in this respect. It is a pity that we could not get such a chance in Delhi. I have received the copy of the letter from China.

A.K. Azad.

(33)

To[1] Jawaharlal Nehru Letter[2] 5th August, 1940

I reached here yesterday from Wardha and hope you have also reached Allahabad by now.

I am writing this letter for two things:

You might remember that we had decided at Poona that Babu Rajendra Prasad should report to the next Working Committee after consultation and due deliberation about the critical situation of the Sugar Factories. But it has become rather difficult owing to the illness of Rajendra Babu. Not only his old ailment has recurred but along with it he is suffering from fever. It had not left him upto the time of my departure from Wardha, and the doctor feared an attack of Pneumonia. I hope he will recover soon but I do not think he would be able to undertake this work so soon. He is advised to take at least one month's complete rest which is indeed very necessary. Under the circumstances we shoutd think out some other method for the above-mentioned work.

If there be no hinderance to do so, I would request you to give some time for this work. Both groups of the Sugar Factory Syndicate are to be consulted. After which, some solution may be evolved on behalf of the Congress. Dr. Katju[3] and Mahmood[4] can supply necessary information to you. Moreover you are already in possession of facts beforehand. If you would not give time, there is none amongst the members of the Working Committee who would do the needful in this matter. I would, then, be forced to undertake this work, and you know that I do not have appropriate temparament for such business.

The second thing is that I wish to go to Allahabad for a few days and spend some time for the office directly. Please let me know where (whether) you are staying in Allahabad or going to Cawanpore. I would not like to disturb your engagements. However if you are staying on in Allahabad these days, I may go there presently; otherwise I may do so after a few days.

I had finished the letter when I came to know that the Governments of Bihar and U.P. have again recognised the Sugar Syndicate. The Government control of the prices has also been decided.

I think that perhaps it is not much necessary for us to consider the matter after this action of the Governments.

A.K. Azad.

(34)

To[1] Lord Linlithgow[2] Telegram[3] 8th August, 1940

Thanks for your Excellency's letter of August fourth and advance copy of declaration received last evening STOP I am thankful for invitation to see you STOP I would have readily availed of pleasure of meeting Your Excellency but when His Majesty's Government have already thought fit to announce a definite line of action may I ask how far there still remains a chance of usefulness of further discussion.

Abul Kalam Azad

(35)

To[1] Lord Linlithgow Telegram[2] 10th August, 1940

Thanks for your Excellency's telegram received through Government House STOP I do not find any meeting ground for Congress in the terms of the declaration of August eight STOP Apart from other fundamental questions there is not even any suggestion for national govèrnment STOP Under the circumstances I am unable to find any scope for further discussion STOP Calling Working Committee eighteenth to consider and decide.

Abul Kalam Azad

(36)

To[1] Lord Linlithgow Letter[2] 11th August, 1940

I had received your Excellency's letter of August 4 on the evening of August 7. As it was necessary to call the Congress Working Committee as soon as possible and to consider any other thing which might be necessary before calling it, I thought it advisible to reply your Excellency's letter telegraphically. Accordingly I sent the following telegram:

(No. 34)

I received your Excellency's second telegram through the Government House Calcutta on Augut 10, in reply to which I sent the following telegram on the same day:

(No. 35)

I would assure you that it would always be a pleasure to me to pay a visit to Your Excellency. When I found that our discussion could not go beyond the terms laid down by the declaration of August 8, I felt that I could not find my way for further discussion.

A.K. Azad

(37)

To[1] Lord Linlithgow Letter[2] 19th August, 1940

As I informed your Excellency in my telegram from Calcutta of the 10th August, I convened a meeting of the Congress Working Committee for the 18th August to consider the statement made on behalf of the British Government. The Committee gave their careful consideration to this statement as well as to the amplification of it in the British Parliament.

The Working Committee will express their views in the course of the next few days dealing with this matter more fully but meanwhile I may inform you that the Committee have read the statements embodying the British Government's decisions and attitude in regard to India with deep regret. These are totally at variance with the proposals last put forward by the Congress at Poona and with the objective of the Congress. The Working Committee are of opinion that they cannot associate themselves in any way with these proposals.

As I ventured to say in my telegram to you, I would have gladly availed of the opportunity to meet you and discuss the whole question. But the terms of the British Government's announcement as well as your communications to me, made it clear that such discussion was to take place within the rigid framework of wholly inadequate proposals and I feel that any discussion on that basis would be fruitless.

I shall be grateful if you will kindly let me know if you have any objection to my releasing our correspondence to the Press.

A.K. Azad

(38)

To[1] Jamnalal Bajaj Telegram[2] 20th December, 1940

Received Jakatdar's letter. Much improved his attitude. Apology accepted. Ban removed.[3]

Abul Kalam Azad

(39)

To[1] Rajendra Prasad Letter[2] 25th December, 1940

I have received today your letter of 21st December and I have received another letter also before it. The matters referred to in your last letter are themselves under my consideration for some time past, specially the matter of local bodies.[3] The Secretary of Purulia Congress Committee had also come here with these questions a few days ago. Undoubtedly it is necessary to have it clearly decided, having all the pros and cons of the problem in view. So far as other provinces are concerned, they are including all such Congressmen in the lists sent to Mahatmaji, who are in the local bodies. And they see the problem in the light of the fact that when we are in the thick of the struggle all other things are of secondary importance, and we should leave them to look after themselves.

However, the decision of all such matters lies with Mahatmaji. You did well in referring the matter to him. I am leaving for Lahore[4] today, from where I shall go to Wardha.[5] I shall fully discuss the matter with Mahatmaji, and let you know the result.

The matter mentioned in your previous letter needs a detailed discussion. I shall try to write to you in detail my journey as soon as I get leisure to do so.

You have written nothing about your health. I hope you are quite well by now.

A.K. Azad.

(40)

To[1] Jawaharlal Nehru Telegram[2] 11th December, 1941

Starting seventeenth direct Bombay Please accompany eighteenth morning Getting one day Bombay and two days Bardoli.

Abul Kalam Azad

(41)

To[1] Jamnalal Bajaj Telegram[2] 11th January, 1942

Despite influenza starting by mail please stop procession or public meeting, if any.

Abul Kalam Azad

(42)

To[1] Jawaharlal Nehru Letter[2] 22nd January, 1942

I have now decided that I will reach Patna on the 30th January, and shall stay there upto the 1st. or the 2nd February Thus I can reach Allahabad on the morning of the 2nd or 3rd February. If you think it to be advisible, you may call a meeting of those members and workers of the Provincial Committee whose presence you deem necessary on the 3rd or the 4th February, in Allahabad.

A.K. Azad

(43)

To[1] Jawaharlal Nehru Letter[2] 27th February, 1942

The Viceroy has announced to celebrate China Day[3] on the 7th of March. The Calcutta Radio informs me that you have given them a message in this connection. They also wish to record my message for broadcasting on the day. Our sympathy with China needs no further elucidation; but would it be a proper way of expression to participate in the function fixed by the Vicerory for their war purposes? I do not think it to be so. I, therefore, could not give a message.

I thought of staying in Allahabad for a day for some office work as well as to meet you. But you were detained in Calcutta and then you had to go direct to Lucknow.

I may probably leave for Wardha on Monday. I could not attend the Shradh of Jumnalalji as the letter sent by

Mahatmaji could not be delivered to me in time and I did not know it. Now I think that I would go there for condolence as soon as possible. Moreover I have to meet Gandhiji also.

There seems to be no immediate need of calling the Working Committee. It may be considered later on.

Rajendra Babu had come here yesterday. We had a detailed talk about the Bihar Congress Committee. I wish he could proceed with it with a firm hand. He has, however, agreed to all my suggestions.

A.K. Azad

(44)

To[1] Jawaharlal Nebru Letter[2] 2nd March, 1942

We have created a Women's Branch in the A.I.C.C. Office but it is not enough. We have to do something more to create practical enthusiasm in the work. I wish to appoint an Advisory Committeee, the members of which may devote their time in this work. I have the following names in view:

Mrs. Pandit[3]
Miss. Mirdulla[4],
Mrs. Asafali[5], and
Mrs. Iftikharuddin.[6]

Including Mrs. Kripalani[7] as the Secretary in charge, this committee would comprise of five members. Please wire your opinion and if you have to suggest any more name, you should certainly do so.

A.K. Azad

(45)

To[1] Friend Circular Letter[2] 3rd March, 1942

Reuter's agency says that the British Premier is going to make a statement about India shortly[3]. We do not know what would be the nature of the statement. Whatever it may be, you would agree with me that, considering the delicacy of the situation, it is advisible to avoid expressing any opinion individually and to wait for the meeting of the Congress Working Committee. The proper place to express our views would be the Committee itself.

A.K. Azad

(46)

To[1] C. Vijiyaraghavacharia Letter[2] 6th March, 1942

Many thanks for your kind letter. Unfortunately the condition is the same as felt by you and every patriotic mind. But there is no alternative before us. We had not demanded power because it was a good occasion to exploit the difficulties of the British Government, we were forced to make this demand because we know that we can not face the coming storm without it. We were convinced that the existing outworn system of the Indian Government was quite unfit to save the country from such a danger. The march of events has clearly demonstrated the truth of our conviction to the world.

We do not want the change of masters[3]. Whether the new master be more bad or less—we have no alternative but to refuse to submit, and die with the satisfaction that we are dying like an honourable man. He who knows how to die, can never feel the sting of helplessness under any circumstances.

You had suggested that in the birth-place of Mahatma Gandhi, a shrine of political pilgrimage be erected. It is a good idea. But do you not feel that such a shrine has already been built in the hearts of millions of Indians, and there is little need of a building made of brick and stones?

With regards and best wishes,

A.K. Azad

(47)

To[1] Jawaharlal Nehru Letter[2] 8th March, 1942

I had already replied your letter[3] when I got your second letter. Previously I had thought that I might go to Wardha for two or three days but the delicate situation of Bengal kept me back and some intricate questions in connection with the Civil Protection[4] could not be left behind unsolved. Now the C.W.C. (Congress Working Committee) is taking place on the 17th, and I am intending to leave for Wardha on the 11th or 12 instant. It would be useful if you could also reach Wardha two days before the 17th. I will let you know of my departure telegraphically.

Badsha Khan[5] sent me several letters to issue a statement as promised at Wardha. After going into all the aspects of the matter, I had to admit that there is no other way but to fulfil his desire. Accordingly a statement has been given to the Press, which you might have seen. I do not know whether you had had correspondence with him in the meantime.

Four or five days ago, a statement of Subhas Babu was broadcast from Berlin and the next day it was announced that it might be heared in his own voice which had been recorded. I heared it. It was the voice of Subhas Babu. I think that probably it was not a record, he himself was speaking. But the broadcast from Tokyo was cartainly a record. The sound of the movement of the record by means of electricity was clearly audible.

The Forward Block ministers Santosh and Banerji are much distressed here; they say that they have not the remotest connection with the Forward Block.

A.K. Azad

(48)

To[1] Rajendra Prasad Telegram[2] 15th March, 1942

Holding Working Committee for important Congress Work.[3] Postponement undesirable. Please attend.

Abul Kalam Azad

(49)

To[1] **PSV (Private Secretary to Viceroy)** **Express Telegram** **19th March, 1942**

Thanks your telegram STOP If Sir Stafford Cripps desires preliminary interchange views I shall gladly meet him STOP My Committee do not consider it necessary to suggest additional names STOP Am proceeding Lahore where my address 21 Aikman Road till twentyfourth STOP From twentyfifth to twentyeighth March expect to be at Anand Bhawan, Allahabad, later Calcutta.

Abul Kalam Azad

(50)

To[1] **B.G. Kher,**[2] **Ravishankar Shukla,**[3] **Biswanathdas,**[4] **Srikrishna Senha.**[5] **Express Telegram**[4] **27th March, 1942**

Understand Cripps invited you STOP May inform him President conducting talks on behalf of Congress as desired by Working Committee STOP If he still wishes see you may meet him after making position clear STOP Ascertain his wishes before starting.

Abul Kalam Azad

(51)

To[1] **Sir Stafford Cripps** **Letter**[2] **1st April, 1942**

I have your letter of today's date for which I thank you. If you so desire it, I shall gladly meet the Commander-in-Chief and Pandit Jawaharlal Nehru will, I hope, be able to accompany me.

My Committee have already arrived at a decision in regard to the proposals communicated by you to us. It was my intention to send this to you this evening or possibly to take it over in person, in case you wished to discuss any point contained in it. This decision naturally covers other points also apart from Defence. I hope to send it to you some time to-day. If you wish to meet again in regard to this I shall gladly meet you.

In your letter you refer to the 'Hindu Press.' I do not know what exactly you mean by this.

A.K. Azad

(52)

To[1] Sir Stafford Cripps[2] Letter[3] 10th April, 1942

On the 2nd April I sent you the resolution of the Working Committee of the Congress containing their views on the tentative proposals put forward by you on behalf of the British Government. In this resolution we expressed our dissent from several important and far-reaching proposals for the future. Further consideration of these proposals has only strengthened us in our conviction in regard to them and we should like to repeat that we cannot accept them as suggested. The Working Committee's resolution gives expression to our conclusions relating to them which we reached after the most earnest consideration.

That resolution, however, emphasized the gravity of the present situation and stated that the ultimate decision that we might take, would be governed by the changes made in the present. The over-riding problem before all of us, and more especially before all Indians, is the defence of the country from aggression and invasion. The future, important as it is, will depend on what happens in the next few months and years We were therefore prepared to do without any assurances for this uncertain future, hoping that through our sacrifices in the defence of our country we would lay the solid and enduring foundations for a free and independent India. We concentrated, therefore, on the present.

Your original proposals in regard to the present, as contained in clause(e) of the proposed declaration were vague and incomplete, except in so far as it was made clear that 'His Majesty's Government must inevitably bear the full responsibility for the defence of India.' These proposals, in effect, asked for participation in the tasks of today with a view to ensure the 'future freedom of India.' Freedom was for an uncertain future, not for the present; and no indication was given in clause (e) of what arrangements or governmental and other changes would be made in the present. When this vagueness was pointed out, you said that this was deliberate, so as to give you freedom to determine these changes in consultation with others. In our talks you gave us to understand that you envisaged a National Government which would deal with all matters except Defence.

Defence at any time, and more particularly in wartime, is of essential importance and without it a National Government functions in a very limited field. Apart from this consideration it was obvious that the whole purpose of your proposals and our talks centred round the urgency of the problems created by the threat of the invasion of India. The chief functions of a National Government must necessarily be to organize Defence both intensively and on the widest popular basis and to create a mass psychology of resistance to an invader. Only a National Government on whom this responsibility was laid, could do this. Popular resistance must have a national background and both the soldier and the civilian must feel that they are fighting for their country's freedom under national leadership.

The question became one not of satisfying our national aspiration but of effective prosecution of the war and fighting to the last any invader who set foot on the soil of India. On general principles a National Government would control Defence through a Defence Minister, and the Commander-in-Chief would control the armed forces and would have full latitude in the carrying out of operations connected with the war. An Indian National Government should have normally functioned in this way. We made it clear that the Commander-in-Chief in India would have control of the armed forces and the conduct of operations and other matters connected therewith. With a view to arriving at a settlement, we were prepared to accept certain limitations on the normal powers of the Defence Minister. We had no desire to upset in the middle of the War the present military organization or arrangements. We accepted also that the higher strategy of the War should be controlled by the War Cabinet in London which would have an Indian member. The immediate object before us was to make the defence of India more effective, to strengthen it, to broadbase it on the popular will and to reduce all red tape, delay and inefficiency from it. There was no question of our interfering with the technical and operational sides. One thing, of course, was of paramount importance to us; India's safety and defence. Subject to this primary consideration there was no reason why there should be any difficulty in finding a way out of the present impase in accordance with the unanimous desire of the Indian people, for in this matter there are no differences amongst us.

The emphasis on Defence led you to reconsider the matter and you wrote to me on the 7th April suggesting a formula for Defence.

In this letter you said, 'As the Working Committee has understood, it is impossible to make any change in the existing constitution during the period of hostilities.' The Working Committee's attitude in the matter has been completely misunderstood and I should like to clear this up, although we are not immediately concerned with it. The Committee do not think that there is any inherent difficulty in the way of constitutional changes during the war. Everything that helps in the War not only can be but must be done, and done with speed. That is the only way to carry on and win a war. No complicated enactments are necessary. A recognition of India's freedom and right to self-determination could easily be made, if it were so wished, together with certain other consequential but important changes. The rest can be left to future arrangements and adjustments. I might remind you that the British Prime Minister actually proposed a union of France and England on the eve of the fall of France. No greater or more fundamental change could be imagined and this was suggested at a period of grave crisis and peril. War accelerates change; it does not fit in with static conceptions.

The formula for Defence that you sent us was considered by us together with its annexure which gave a list of subjects or departments which were to be transferred to the Defence Department. This list was a revealing one as it proved that the Defence Minister would deal with relatively unimportant matters. We were unable to accept this and we informed you accordingly.

Subsequently, a new formula for Defence was suggested to us, but without any list of subjects. This formula seemed to us to be based on a more healthy approach and we suggested certain changes pointing out that our ultimate decision would necessarily depend on the allocation of subjects. A revised formula was then sent back to us together with an indication of the functions of the War Department.

This was so widely and comprehensively framed that it was difficult for us to know what the actual allocation of subjects and departments, as between the Defence Department and the War Department, would be. A request was made on our behalf that illustrative lists of these subjects might be supplied to enable us to consider the matter. No such lists were supplied to us.

In the interview we had with you yesterday we discussed the new formula and expressed our view-point in regard to it. I need not repeat what I said then. The wording of the formula is after all a minor matter and we should not allow that to come in our way, unless some important principle is at stake. But behind that wording lay certain ideas and we were surprised to find that during the past few days we had been proceeding on wrong assumptions.

When we asked you for illustrative lists of subjects for the two departments, you referred us to the old list for the Defence Department which you had previously sent us and which we had been unable to accept. You added that certain residuary subjects might be added to this but, in effect, there was not likely to be any such subject as the allocation was complete. Thus, you said, that substantially there was no change between the old list and any new one that might be prepared. If this was so, and we were to go back ultimately to the place we started from, then what was the purpose of our searching for a new formula? A new set of words meaning the same thing made no difference. In the course of our talks many other matters were also cleared up, unfortunately to our disadvantage. You had referred both privately and in the course of public statements to a National Government and a 'Cabinet' consisting of 'ministers.' These words have a certain significance and we had imagined that the new Government would function with full powers as a cabinet, with the Viceroy acting as a constitutional head. But the new picture that you placed before us was really not very different from the old, the difference being one of degree and not of kind. The Government could neither be called except vaguely and inaccurately, nor could it function as a National Government. It would just be the Viceroy and his Executive Council with the Viceroy having all his old powers. We did not ask for any legal changes but we did ask for definite assurances and conventions which would indicate that the new Government would function as a free government, the members of which act as members of a cabinet in a constitutional government. In regard to the conduct of the War and connected activities the Commander-in-Chief would have freedom and he would act as War Minister.

We were informed that nothing can be said at this stage, even vaguely and generally, about the conventions that should govern the Government and the Viceroy. Ultimately there was always the possibility of the members of the Executive Council resigning or threatening to resign if they disagreed with the Viceroy. That sanction or remedy is of course always open but it is curious that we should base our approach to a new government on the probability of conflict and resignation at the very outset.

The picture, therefore, placed before us is not essentially different from the old one. The whole object which we, and I believe you have in view—that is, to create a new psychological approach to the people, to make them feel that their own national government had come, that they were defending their newly-won freedom—would be completely frustrated when they saw this old picture again, with even the old labels on. The continuation of the India Office which has been a symbol of evil to us, would confirm this picture. It has almost been taken for granted for some time past that the India Office would soon disappear as it was an anachronism. But now we are told that even this undesirable relic of a past age is going to continue.

The picture of the government, which was so like the old in all essential features, is such that we cannot fit into it. Normally we could have had little difficulty in disposing of this matter for it is so far removed from all that we have striven for but in the circumstances of today we were prepared to give full consideration to every proposal which might lead to an effective organization of the defence of India. The peril that faces India affects us more than it can possibly affect any foreigner, and we are anxious and eager to do our utmost to face it and overcome it. But we cannot undertake responsibilities when we are not given the freedom and power to shoulder them effectively and when an old environment continues which hampers the national effort.

While we cannot accept the proposals you have made, we want to inform you that we are yet prepared to assume responsibility provided a truly national government is formed. We are prepared to put aside for the present all questions about the future, though as we have indicated, we hold definite views about it. But in the present, the National Government must be a cabinet government with full power and must not merely be a continuation of the Viceroy's Executive Council. In regard to defence we have already stated what, in our opinion, the position should be at present. We feel that such an arrangement is the very minimum that is essential for the functioning of a National Government and for making the popular appeal which is urgently needed.

We would point out to you that the suggestions we have put forward are not ours only but may be considered to be the unanimous demand of the Indian people. On these matters there is no difference of opinion among the various groups and parties, and the difference is as between the Indian people as a whole and the British Government. Such differences as exist in India relate to constitutional changes in the future. We are agreeable to the postponement of this issue so that the largest possible measure of unity might be achieved in the present crisis for the defence of India. It would be a tragedy that even when there is this unanimity of opinion in India, the British Government should prevent a free National Government from functioning and from serving the cause of India as well as the larger causes for which millions are suffering and dying today.

A.K. Azad

(53)

To[1] Sir Stafford Cripps, Letter[2] 11th April, 1942

I have just received your letter of April 10th and I must confess that my colleagues and I were considerably surprised to read it. I am sending you this reply immediately and can only deal briefly here with some of the points you have raised.

The points covered by our original resolution are important and represent my Committee's well-considered views on the British proposals as a whole. But we pointed out to you that so far as proposals relate to the future they might be set aside, as we were anxious to assume responsibility for India's government and defence in this hour of danger. This responsibility could only be undertaken, however, if it was real responsibility and power.

As regards the division of functions between the Defence Minister and the War Minister you did not givc illustrative lists, as requested by us, and referred us to the previous list of the Defence Minister's functions, which, as you know, we had been wholly unable to accept. In your letter under reply you mention certain subjects, directly or indirectly related to the War, which will be administered by other departments. So far as the Defence Minister is concerned, it is clear that his functions will be limited by the first list that you sent.

No one has suggested any restrictions on the normal powers of the Commander-in-Chief. Indeed we went beyond this and were prepared to agree to further powers being given to him as War Minister. But it is clear that the British Government's conception and ours in regard to defence differ greatly. For us it means giving it a national character and calling upon every man and woman in India to participate in it. It means trusting our people and seeking their full co-operation in this great effort. The British Government's view seems to be based on an utter lack of confidence in the Indian people and in withholding real power from them. You refer to the paramount duty and responsibility of His Majesty's Government in regard to defence. That duty and responsibility cannot be discharged effectively unless the Indian people are made to have and feel their responsibility, and the recent past stands witness to this. The Government of India do not seem to realize that the War can only be fought on a popular basis.

Your statement that we have for the first time after three weeks suggested a change in the constitution is hardly correct. In the course of our talks reference was made to it, but it is true that we did not lay stress on it as we did not want to introduce new issues. But when you stated explicitly in your letter that we had agreed that no constitutional changes could be made during the war, we had to deny this and correct your impression.

It is the last part of your letter that has especially surprised and pained us. It seems that there has been a progressive deterioration in the British Government's attitude as our negotiation proceeded. What we were told in our first lalk with you is now denied or explained away. You told me then that there would be a National Government which would function as a Cabinet and that the position of the Viceroy should be analogous to that of the King in England vis-a-vis his Cabinet. In regard to the India Office, you told me, that you were surprised that no one had so far mentioned this important matter and that the practical course was to have this attached or incorporated with the Dominion's Office.

The whole of this picture which you sketched before us has now been completely shattered by what you told us during our last interview.

You have put forward an argument in your letter which at no time during our talks was mentioned by you. You refer to the 'absolute dictatorship of the majority'. It is astonishing that such a statement should be made in this connection and at this state. This difficulty is inherent in any scheme of a mixed cabinet formed to meet an emergency, but there are many ways in which it can be provided for. Had you raised this question we would have discussed it and found a satisfactory solution. The whole approach to this question has been that a mixed cabinet should be formed and should co-operate together. We accepted this. We are not interested in the Congress as such gaining power, but we are interested in the Indian people as a whole having freedom and power. How the Cabinet should be formed and should function was a question which might have been considered after the main question was decided; that is, the extent of power which the British Government would give up to the Indian people. Because of this we never discussed it with you or even referred to it. Nevertheless you have raised this matter for the first time, in what is presumably your last letter to us, and tried most unjustifiably to sidetrack the real issue between us.

You will remember that in my very first talk with you, I pointed out that the communal or like questions did not axise at this stage. As soon as the British Government made up its mind to transfer real power and responsibility, the other questions could be tackled successfully by those concerned. You gave me the impression that you agreed with this approach.

We are convinced that if the British Government did not pursue a policy of encouraging disruption, all of us, to whatever party or group we belonged, would be able to come together and find a common line of action. But, unhappily, even in this grave hour of peril, the British Government is unable to give up its wrecking policy. We are driven to the conclusion that it attaches more importance to holding on to its rule in India, as long as it can, and promoting discord and disruption here with that end in view, than to an effective defence of India against the aggression and invasion that overhang us. To us, and to all Indians, the dominant consideration is the defence and safety of India, and it is by that test that we judge.

You mention that you propose to public your letter to me. I presume that you have no objection now to our publishing our original resolution, your letters to us, and our letters to you.

A.K. Azad.

(54)

To[1] Dr. B.C. Roy Telegram[2] 28th April, 1942.

Government India granted permission our sending medical unit[3] Manipur road for employment in camps between Tamu and Sittaung inside Burma Stop Evacuation authorities. Assam suggest party about eight doctors eight compounders and personal servants two sanitary inspectors with one months medical store and equipment on basis 300 daily cases subsequent medical stores being supplied from Government stock Imphal Stop. Government promise all facilities requires seven days notice before unit leaves stop. Please take immediate steps organise unit in cooperation relief societies Stop. Wire estimate expenditure and likely date departure unit Stop. Issuing appeal funds.

Abul Kalam Azad.

(55)

To[1] J.B. Kripalani Letter[2] 7th May, 1942.

You might have received my last letter. I do not know whether the office has received any donations in connection with my appeal for the Medical Mission. If it has received any, please arrange it to be sent to me. Moreover please inform Messrs Bachhraj & Co., Bombay to send all the amount received in this connection direct on my Calcutta address. Money for expenses is urgently needed.

A.K. Azad.

(56)

To[1] Jawaharlal Nehru Letter[2] 9th May, 1942.

I do not know whether you received my letter sent to you care of the U.P.P.C.C.; Lucknow. An important matter was mentioned in the letter. You might have received the reply to your Lucknow letter on reaching Lahore.

I have received a letter from Bapu.[3] He wants me to see him. The papers say that he is leaving for Bombay for a week. I am, therefore, intending to leave for Bombay on Monday or Tuesday. The selfish feeling of taking rest is to a certain extent working behind this intention. The weather of Bombay would after all be less oppressive to me than that of Wardha.

Bapu also mentioned in his letter that you may also meet him if possible; but I do not think that there is any need for it at present.

If this need will be felt after the Bombay meeting, then an occasion may arise by the end of this month, after your return from Kulu.

I shall stay at Bholabhai's in Bombay, and if possible I might go for a day or two to Juhu.

Please convey my *salams* to Mrs. and Mr. Iftikhar. I have received letters of Rajendra Babu and Patel also.

A.K. Azad.

(57)

To[1] Jawaharlal Nehru Letter[2] 13th May, 1942.

I thank you for the telegram and the letter you have sent to me from Delhi. Please note that I have said, "I thank you",

I have not said only 'thanks'. Thus I have fully kept up the subtle distinction between the two modes of expression which you had indicated to me in Delhi.

I have received a letter from Kidwai[3] and Paliwal[4] has also wired to me his readiness in connection of (with) the evacuation of children. I am settling the details with the Bengal Government. As soon as they reach a definite point, I shall inform the U.P. friends.

But I came to know to-day that Kidwai has yesterday been arrested suddenly under the Defence of India Act. I am at a loss to understand what has he done within the last few days that he has become a dangerous man anew for the U.P. Government.

I had written to you in my last letter that I was leaving for Bombay. But the affairs of Bengal have stuck to me in such a way that I had to postpone my visit. The Chittagong air attack[5] has created a feeling here that Calcutta will also be attacked within a few days. Moreover new and difficult problems have suddenly arisen in connection with the coastal population of Bengal. Under the circumstances I could not prepare myself to go out.

It pains me to find that Iftikhar is going out of the way.[6] I do not know whether you tried to bring him round and with what result.

The longer you stay at Kulu, the happier shall I be. I was much concerned to find you depressed in Allahabad. Now you should admit that you are going towards the wrong side of fifty and you should be a little more careful about your health.

A.K. Azad.

(58)

To[1] J.B. Kripalani Letter[2] 20th May, 1942.

I had written to you to send me without delay all the donations received directly in the office about the Congress Medical Mission and to write to Messrs Bachhraj Co., to send me all the amount received in this connection. In reply Mr. Sadikali[3] wrote that arrangements had been made about it. But more than a week has elasped and I have received neither the amount sent by the office nor from Bombay.

I do not understand the cause of delay. Kindly send me all the amount received under this head.

My travelling and office bills have already been sent. I am waiting for their clearance also.

Hope you are doing well.

A.K. Azad.

(59)

To[1] Jawaharlal Nehru Letter[2] 22nd May, 1942.

It seems that my letters to you on the Kulu address did not reach you otherwise you would have known that I had cancelled my journey to Bombay and you would not have wired to me there. I am sorry that you had to wire to Bombay owing to have missed my letters.

I want to meet Bapu alone first and then we may meet him together. I shall leave for Wardha as soon as the urgent Bengal affairs allow me to do so. In the meanwhile, I request you to spare some time for Madras, if there be no other pressing engagement. You had told me in Allahabad that you would do so. It is necessary from every point of view. I would be thankful to you, if you could leave for Madras after staying in Allahabad for a few days. Thus on your return from Madras you can break journey at Wardha.

It is also possible that if you could leave sooner for Madras, I may reach Wardha a few days before the probable date of your return from Madras and then we may meet there.

A.K. Azad.

(60)

To[1] J.B. Kripalani Letter[2] 23rd May 1942.

Sometime in the year before last the attention of the

office was drawn to the fact that the title head of office letter papers should be uniform in both Hindustani and English. The All India Congress Committee is not only known to the remotest villager but it has become an international term. Moreover it is wrong on (in) principle to translate proper nouns in other languages. Since the very time, the Congress came into existence, its name is Indian National Congress; we cannot adopt another name for it, unless the Congress itself changes it.[8] But in Nagri script it has been translated into Akhil Bharatiya Congress Committee. Please get it changed into All India Congress Committee in Nagri character also. If we change the name in Nagri characters, it becomes necessary to do the same in Urdu characters. If this is done, the same organisation will be called by three different names. This would be not only wrong but ridiculous. Names are never translated.

Only two writing pads were sent by the office last month. Please instruct them to send a few more. The paper used is rather thick and carbon copies become faint. If possible, thinner paper might be used for some pads. But the first thing to be done is to have one name only in all the three characters. I hope you will pay immediate attention to this matter.

A.K. Azad.

(61)

To[1] J.B. Kripalani Letter[2] 27th May, 1942.

All of a sudden I read in the newspapers that the A.I.C.C. Office has sent Dr. Lohia[3] to Calcutta, to inspect and report about Bengal P.C.C. Yesterday he came to me, and on inquiry he told me that he was coming here on private business and therefore he also took this work into his hand.

I like Lohia from the beginning. It would be good if he could attach himself to Congress Office. But I regret to say that his present procedure for which you too gave him a sanction, is extremely objectionable. If some one goes somewhere for his private business, it does not necessarily follow that he should be charged with the inspection of a Provincial Committee, and thus create misunderstanding among the people unnecessarily. Long articles are appearing in Calcutta papers criticising and expressing surprise over this episode.

There are two ways of inspecting the P.C.C.'s for the Central Office. One way is to keep constantly in touch with them, and the work of (inspection) should go on in the usual way. The other way is to send some responsible person on an extra-ordinary inspection to a particular P.C.C., which means that the office has some grievances about it which needs inquiry. Please note that if it be necessary in future to make inspection or inquiry of the latter kind, it should not be done without the knowledge of the President.

Please consider how much objectionable it is to send a man to Bengal without informing me, despite the fact that I am present here.

Please let me know by return post, how the matter of Dr. Lohia's being sent here happened. It happened by your knowledge, or it is the work of some one else in the office. I am leaving for Wardha on the 29th. Please reply on Wardha address.

A.K. Azad.

(62)

To[1] Jawaharlal Nehru Letter[2] 31st May, 1942.

Your letter of 27th May from Wardha had reached me day before yesterday. I am sending this letter to Allahabad so that you may get it as soon as you reach there.

When you were staying in Calcutta en-route to Assam, you might remember that one day I had a sudden attack of giddiness while talking to you. At Allahabad too this had happened once,[3] but I did not take any notice of it. Recently it has recurred many a time, specially when I work long. The remedy seems to be, that I should give up the work for a few days and take rest but you know the circumstances cannot permit me to do so. Even if I am allowed to do so, how would it be possible to take rest after leaving work ?

I am much disturbed over certain matters. I do not know

what are your feelings now. My mind seems to be much oppressed, which burden I cannot remove in any way.

You write that you will be ready after the 3rd June. Owing to my present state of health, I think, I shall not be able to leave on the 4th. I might be delayed for a few days. However, it is certain that we have to go to Wardha next week. If my complaint does not increase, I may probably be able to leave on the 5th or 6th instant. In any case I shall let you know by telegram before-hand so that you may also be able to leave Allahabad the same day.

The Medical Mission is working in Silchar satisfactorily. The local responsible men are praising its work. A number of refugees are coming to Goalundo. A Unit has, therefore, been sent there also. Kiran Sankar Roy[4] is going there for its opening ceremony.

The refugees from Burma are also pouring in Sylhet and Karimganj. Most of them succumb to epidemic diseases. The local Congress Committee had made arrangements for doctors. They were in need of medicines, clothes, and male-nurses which we have supplied them.

Owing to the air raid by Japan on the borders of Assam, a new situation has arisen in the whole province. People leave the cities for villages where owing to rains a great danger of seasonal diseases is imminent. Moreover, the Marwari grain dealers have totally vacated the province which has caused great dislocation of grain business. There is no purchaser of the Assam paddy and no one is there to supply them with other kinds of grains which are needed by Assam. The military is purchasing away all the local stock of medicines, and there is a great dearth of necessary medicines.

These conditions require our utmost vigilance to relieve the distress of Assam. I have done whatever I possibly could immediately and I hope I shall be able to help them sufficiently from Calcutta.

A.K. Azad.

(63)

To[1] Jawaharlal Nehru Letter[2] 6th June, 1942.

I am in receipt of your letter of 2nd June[3] and I got your telegram also.[4] I wonder why my letters do not reach you. As you were reaching Allahabad on the 1st June, I had despatched a letter on 31st May to your Allahabad address so that you may get (it) as soon as you reach there. Later on I sent another letter on 3rd June, in which I have informed you that I was leaving for Wardha on the 8th June and hoped that you would also be able to proceed the same day.

You have been writing to me from every place you visited in your tour. I am thankful to you for the same. I had similarly tried to keep you informed of my activities constantly but it seems that you got my letters upto Lahore after which you somehow missed them. I had written two letters to your Kulu address.

Probably the letters are now-a-days delayed owing to censorship and perhaps they are lost also. Please ask the servants of Anand Bhavan about my letter of May 31 which might have been misplaced.

Owing to the matters connected with the Medical Mission my departure to Wardha was delayed for three or four days. The Government of Assam had put certain obstacles in the smooth working of the Mission in Slichar. I was, therefore, prepared to withdraw it. But they are, after all, now being removed by the intervention of General Wood.[5] He has further requested the Congress to send a complete Unit with fifty volunteers to Dimapur also. I am, therefore, arranging to send it. Dr. Roy is taking rest in Shillong.

However, I am leaving for Wardha on the 8th June,[6] and I hope that you would also be able to proceed on the 8th.

I am sorry that you were troubled on not receiving my letters but you may realise that it is not my fault.

A.K. Azad.

PART II

Statements and Appeals

(64)

Extracts from the English Translation[1] of Maulana Azad's Urdu Statement before[2] the Court.

"I had no intention of submitting here any statement oral or written. This is a place in which there is for us no hope, no demand, and no grievance of any sort. This is a turn, without passing through which, we cannot reach our goal...Non-Cooperation[3] is essentially the result of absolute desperation at existing circumstances...I want to make it quite distinct that the term Non-Cooperation applies only to the Government, its administrative system and its executive and political principles and not to any persons or individuals.

"Like most occurrences of the present era this movement also is nothing novel. History bears ample testimony to the fact that whenever a ruling authority has taken up arms against liberty and truth, courts of justice have lent themselves admirably to purposes of a most facile and unfailing weapon for the practice of such inequity. The authority of the law courts is a power which can be used equally to do justice and to perpetuate injustice. In the hands of an equitable Government they are the best instruments of justice and truth; but in the hands of tyrannical and autocratic Government no weapon is deadlier than these for purposes of revenge and inequity. No pure-minded and truth-loving section of humanity can be found, including even the inventors and savants of science, which has not some time or other stood in the dock before a court of law...

"The inequities of courts of law constitute an endless list and history has not yet finished singing the elegy of such miscarriages of justice. In that list we observe a holy personage like Jesus who had to stand in his time before a foreign court, convicted even as the worst of criminals. We see also in the same list Socrates who was sentenced to be poisoned for no other crime than that of being the most truthful person of his age. We meet also the name of that great Florentine martyr to truth, the inventor Gallileo, who refused to belie his observations and researches merely because their avowal was a crime in the eyes of constituted authority...When I ponder on the great and significant history of the convicts' dock and find that the honour of standing in that place belongs to me to-day, my soul becomes steeped in thankfulness and praise of God[4]...

"The bureaucracy in India is nothing more nor less than the domination which powerful individuals will always normally attain over a nation decaying by its own neglect and internal weaknesses. In the natural course of things such dominant authority cannot possibly countenance any nationalistic awakening or agitations for progress, reform or justice. And as such agitation would spell the inevitable downfall of its dominant power, it seeks to kill all agitation by declaring it a crime against constituted authority. No power would tamely submit to movements likely to bring about its own decline, however much such decline might be in the ultimate interests of justice. This posture of affairs is merely a struggle for existence in which both sides fight desparately for their principles. An awakened nation aspires to attain what it considers its birthright and the dominant authority would fain not budge an inch from its position of unquestioned sway. The contention might almost be advanced that the latter party even like its opponents is not open to any blame in as much as it is merely putting up a fight for its own survival and it is quite an incidental matter that its existence happens to be inimical to perpetuation of justice. We cannot deny facts of human nature and its inseparable characteristics. Like good, evil also desires to live in this world and struggle for its own existence. In India also such a struggle for the survival of the fittest has already commenced. Most certainly, therefore, nothing can be a higher crime against the domination of Government, as at present established, than the agitation which seeks to terminate its unlimited authority in the name of liberty and justice. I fully admit that I am not only guilty of such agitation in the heart of our nation and dedicated their whole lives to the cherishing and breeding of this holy discontent...

"The history of politics teaches us that foolishness and recklessness of consequences are always the companions of a decadent power. The Government thought that by sheer repression it would innihilate the Khilafat[5] and the Swaraj[6] movements and stop the hartal of the 24th. Accordingly it declared the Volunteer Corps to be unlawful and many workers were indiscriminately arrested. It fancied that the Khilafat and the Congress Committees would become inane and inactive by the mere arrest of the executive and the prohibition of the Volunteer Corps. Thus would the hartal be automatically stopped. But very soon the Government came to learn that repression when practised against national awakening is no fatal thing for a nation but instead breathes new life into it. Neither was the hartal stopped, nor did the Khilafat and the Congress Committee become moribund, nor was the work of the volunteer stopped even for a single day...

"According to my belief it is my duty to speak out at the present moment and I cannot fall short of the full performance of my duty, just because it might be construed into a crime...Most certainly I have stated that the present Government is oppressive. If I do not say this, what else am I to say? I fail to understand why it should be expected of me that I should call things by any but their right names. I refuse absolutely to call black white...I have certainly been asserting that only two paths are open to us in this matter of our duty. The Government has to refrain from all this inequity and deprivation of liberty; or if it cannot bring itself to do so, it has to be wiped off...I believe in the evils of the present Government most assuredly. I could not at the same time pray that it may not mend its ways and yet be long lived...

"Now what is the reason that such is the firm beiief of myself and of millions of my countrymen? The reasons for this have now become so patent to common knowledge that in the words of Milton, 'Next to the Sun itself they are about the clearest and most manifest fact in existence.' About such universal facts all that I can say is don't deny them. I will only add that this faith of mine exists because I am an Indian, because I am a Muslim and first and last because I am a man.

"It is my belief that liberty is the natural and God-given right of man. No man and no bureaucracy consisting of men has got the right to make the servants of God its own slaves. However attractive be the euphemism invented for 'subjugation' and 'slavery', still slavery is slavery and it is opposed to the will and to the canons of God. I therefore do not consider the bureaucracy of India to be a legitimate sovereign and I consider it a bounden duty to liberate country from its yoke. The notorious fallacies of 'Reform' and 'gradual transference of powers' can produce no illusions and pitfalls in my unequivocal and definite faith. Liberty being the primary right of man, it is nobody's personal privilege to prescribe limits or apportion shares in the distribution of it. To say that a nation should get its liberty in graduated stages is the same as saying that an owner should by right receive his property only in bits and a creditor his dues by instalments...Whatever philanthrophic acts might be performed by a man who has usurped our property, his usurpation would still continue to be utterly illegal.

"Evil cannot be classified into good and bad. All that is in fairness possible is to fix its gradations with respect to quality. For instance we can say very heinous robbery and less heinous robbery, but who can speak of good robbery and bad robbery? I cannot, therefore, at all conceive of any justification for such domination because by its very nature it is an act of inequity...

"Such is my duty as a man and as an Indian and religious injunctions have also taught me the same lesson. In fact in my view the greatest proof of the truth of my religion is that it is another name for the teaching of the rights of man. I am a Muslim and by virtue of being a Muslim this has become my religious duty. Islam never accepts as valid a sovereignty which is personal or is constituted of a bureaucuracy of a handful of paid executive. Islam constitutes a perfected system of freedom and democracy. It has been sent down to get back for the human race the liberty which has been snatched away from it. Monarchs, foreign dominations, selfish religious pontiffs and powerful sections had alike misappropriated this liberty of man. They had been fondly nursing the belief that power and possession spell the highest right is not might but right itself. No one except God has got the right. The moment Islam appeared it proclaimed that the highest right is not might but right itself. No one except God has got the right to make serfs and slaves of God's creatures. All men are equal and their fundamental rights are on a par. He only is greater than others, whose deeds are the most righteous of all...

"The sovereignty of the Prophet of Islam and of the Khalif was a perfected conception of democratic equality and it only could take shape with the whole nation's free will, unity, suffrage and election. This is the reason why the sovereign or president of a republic is like a designated Khalif; Khilafat literally means nothing more nor less than a representation; so that all the authority a Khalif possesses consists in his representative character and he possesses no domination beyond this representative authority.

"If then Islam defines it as a duty of Muslims to refuse to acknowledge the moral justification even of an Islamic Government, if full play is not granted in it to the will and franchise of the nation, it is perfectly superfluous to add what under Islam would be the ruling given about a foreign bureaucracy. If to-day there was to be established in India an Islamic Government but if the system of that Government was based upon personal monarchy or upon bureaucratic oligarchy, then to protest against the existence of such a Government would still be my primary duty as a Muslim. I would still call the Government oppressive and demand its replacement.

"I frankly confess that this original conception of Islamic sovereignty could not be uniformly maintained in its primal purity on account of the selfishness and personal domineering of the later Muslim sovereigns. The mighty magnificence of the Emperors of ancient Rome and of the Shahs of Persia had attraeted the Muslim sovereigns powerfully to the dubious glory of great monarchical empires. They began to prefer the majestic figures of a Kaiser or a Khosroe to the simple dignity of the original Khalifs clad often times in old tatered cloaks. No period of the dynastic sovereignties of Islam has however failed to produce some true Muslim martyrs who have made public deflarations of the tyrannies and transgressions of such monarchies and had joyfully and triumphantly suffered all miseries and hardships which inevitably confronted them in the thorny paths of duty.

"The holy prophet of Islam has preached the following doctrine to the Muslims: 'The man is blessed with the best of deaths who proclaims the truth in the face of a tyrannical administration and is sluaughtered in punishment of this deed.' Scripture of Islam, the holy Quran, defines the greatest attribute of the true Muslims to be 'that they fear not any being except God and whatever they consider to be 'that they fear not any being except God and whatever they consider to be the truth, they reck not any authority in the public proclamation of such truth.' The Quran further defines the national characteristics of the Muslim as follows: 'They are the witnesses to truth on God's earth.' As long therefore, as they continue to be Muslims they can not desist from giving this public evidence. In fact it has designated Muslims as witnesses i.e. givers of the evidence of truth. When the prophet of Islam extracted a promise of righteousness from any person, one of the clauses of such a bond used to be. 'I will always proclaim the truth in whatever condition and wherever I may happen to be.'...

"An outstanding object lesson in speaking the truth which their national history presents to the Muslims is to be found in the order of an autocratic monarch by which each organ of a victim's body was cut off. The charge against the victim was that he had proclaimed the iniquity of the tyrant. Firm as a rock he stood and took his punishment in all its heinous stages but his tongue right on to the moment when it was severed went on proclaiming that autocrat was a tyrant, This is an incident of the reign of the Emperor Abdul Malik whose domain extended from Syria to Sind. Can any one then attach any weight to a sentence under Section 124 as compared to this terrible penalty? I concede that it is the moral decadence of Muslims and their renouncing the real Islamic life that is responsible for the bringing about of this fallen state.

"While I am penning these lines I know their is still living in India many a Muslim who through his weakness pays homage to this very tyranny. But the failure of man to act up to the spirit of certain tenets can not belie the intrinsic truth of those principles.

"The tenets of Islam are preserved in its scriptures. This under no circumstances make it permissible for Muslims to enjoy life at the expense of liberty. A true Muslim has either to immolate himself or to retain his liberty, no other course is open for him under his religion. To-day the Muslims have come to a firm decision that in freering their country from its slavery they will take their fullest share along with their Hindu, Sikh, Parsi and Christian breathern...It is now their belief that to axpect any justice from the British Government would be nothing but pure self-deception so that if they really aspire to obtain justice there is only one single avenue leading to it which is the attainment of Swaraj-meaning the Government of India for India and by the Indians themselves.[4] In short on these points my admissions have ever been absolutely clear and unequivocal.

"The present Government is a most illegitimate form of bureaucracy. It is openly spurning the wishes and aspirations of millions of humanity. It has always given the preference over justice to prestige...Does tyranny acquire a right to be given a different name simply because it happens to be powerful and to possess jails?

"In the words of the good and truthful national hero of Italy, Joseph Mazzini, I repeat 'we cannot possibly deny your evil doings just because temporal power happens to be your possession for a time,...

"Continuously in the last twelve years I have been training my commmunity and my country in demanding their rights and the liberty.[7] I was only 18 years old when I first started speaking and writing on this theme.[8] I have consecrated my whole being to it and sacrificed the best part of my life, meaning the whole of my youth in my infatuation for this ideal.

For four years I have suffered internment but doing my internment even. I have never desisted from pushing on my work and inviting people to this national goal.[9] This is the perennial mission of my life and if I live at all I select to live only for this single purpose. Even as the Quran says, 'My prayers and my observances and my life and my death are all for my Lord, the God of the Universe. I am the first pioneer in this latest phase of that Islamic movement in India which has created a tremendous revolution in the political world of the Indian Muslims and has gradually elevated them to the pinnacle of national consciousness on which they are seen to-day. In 1912 I started an Urdu journal, the *Al-Hilal*[10], which was the organ of this movement and the object of the publication of which was mainly that I have declared above. It is an actual faet that within the three years it had created a new atmosphere in the religious and the political life of Muslims of India.

"In this war of liberty and justice, I have adopted the path of non-violent non-cooperation. Opposed to us stands an authority armed with the complete equipment for oppression, excess and bloodshed. But we place our relianee and trust, next to God, only on our own limitless power of sacrifice and unshakeable fortitude.

"Unlike Mahatma Gandhi, my belief is not that armed force should never be opposed by armed force. It is my belief that such opposing of violence with violence is fully in harmony with the natural laws of God in those circumstances under which Islam permits the use of such violence.[11] But at the same time for purpose of liberation of India at the present agitation, I entirely agree with all the arguments of Mahatma Gandhi and I have complete confidence in his honesty. It is my definite conviction that India cannot attain success by means of arms nor is it advisable for it to adopt that course. India can only triumph through non-violent agitation and India's triumph will be a memorable example of the victory of moral force.

"This is the reason why I have always preached to the masses peaceful agitation and have invariably prescribed it as the first postulate of success. This would appear distinctly from these speeches also. I am one of the handful of Muslim leaders who can honestly claim that if it was not for the determined and effective control that they have exercised in keeping the Muslim public within the bounds of non-cooperation, there is no knowing where the excitement of the mobs, under the recent trying provocations, may not have led them and what grave situations may not have taken shape with respect to the Khailafat problem.

"What I have stated in the beginning I will repeat in conclusion, that what the Government is doing with us to-day is no extraordinary procedure for which it can be particularly blameable. It is second nature to every usurping authority to put up a determined opposition and repression, to supress national awakening and we know that human nature cannot be altered to suit our own end. This natural failing finds expression equally in individuals and communities. How many people are there in this world who would give back any article which they had already got in their possession for the mere reason that they are not legitimately entitled to it? How then can we nurse a fond hope of such voluntary surrender with respect to a whole continent? Power also is not normally prone to admit facts just because they are logical and proved. As a matter of fact it waits for the emergence of a counter-strength and when this does present itself, it bows its head down before the most improper demand. Patience, therefore, and a tug of war of strength are unavoidable,

"This position is one which should be accepted as a normal and everyday occurence without surprise and without demur. I will even go the length of admitting that the present repression is certainly not too drastic as compared to the worst instances of inhuman oppressions and terrible persecutions which history presents to us. I am not quite certain whether this is due to immaturity of the national sense of sacrifice or the imperfect development of the present system of repression. The future alone will decide this. Just as the beginning of such political tug of war has uniformly been on more or less similar lines, even so its end has been the same in the history of all nations. I know that if our spirit of liberty and justice proves by actual demonstration to be real and unconquerable, this very Government which is to-day putting us into the dock, will be obliged to give us a right royal reception as triumphant patriots......

Before I conclude my statement, I want to say a few words about those countrymen of mine who are working against me in this prosecution. Previously I have stated somewhere that the work of the C.I.D. is a combination of ignorance and trickery. This I have said from the personal experience that I have gained from countless prosecutions. All the same, however, I admit that all the C.I.D. people who have given evidence against me have not deliberately made any lying statements, barring perhaps the confidence which they have expressed in their own work......I believe that the confidence which they have expressed on the results of their own work and the motives which have dectated their actions are certainly sinful. But at the same time I also know their weakness. They are only doing this for the sake of the appointments which bring them a few rupees and their only crime is that they do not possess the moral courage to give preference to truth over everything else. In my heart, therefore, lingers no rancour or accusation.

(65)

Joint Statement by Maulana Azad and other Congress Leaders on the situation in the Punjab.[1] (4th May, 1923)

In response to the repeated, pressing invitations from leading Congressmen in the province, we arrived in the Punjab at different times during the latter half of March and the first week of April. It had been impressed upon us that the communal differences in the Punjab had arrived at a state which demanded the undivided attention of public men in India and the immediate presence of some of them on the spot. On arrival here we found that the relations between the Hindus and Mussulmans, both educated and uneducated, were so greatly strained that each community as a whole had practically arrayed itself in an armed camp against the other.[2]

Causes of Strife

Since our arrival in the Punjab we have individually and

collectively made careful enquiries into the true causes of this unfortunate state of things. The conclusion at which we have arrived is that, while it is true that almost the whole Hindu and Mussulman population of the Punjab is, more or less, affected, the reasons which apply to the so-called educated classes are entirely different from those which apply to the masses, and we feel constrained to say that the latter have to no small extent been exploited by interested persons among the former for their own selfish ends. So far as regards the masses, the real causes of the trouble are, firstly, the memories of Malabar[3] and the Multan riots. Secondly, the Shuddhi[4] and the Hindu Sanghatan[5] movements which have in their turn given rise to counter agitation amongst the Mohammedans. These movements, we are sorry to say, are being carried on in spirit of hostility which has been fostered and spread throughout the province and beyond it by the press of both communities. We have tried our best to explore all possible avenues leading to a restoration of good feeling but have unfortunately not met with a satisfactory measure of success.

We shall first deal with the disruptive elements which affect the two communities generally. Malabar is but a sad memory which is only relevant to our present purpose in so far as the origin of the mischief is traceable to it. No practical steps in that connection are necessary except to impress upon the Press and the people the utter futility of continuing to harp upon the deplorable events associated with that unfortunate part of the country. The case with the Multan riots is, however, different as the wounds inflicted are comparatively fresh.

Multan

Three of us (Maulana Azad, Pandit Motilal Nehru and Mrs. Sarojini Naidu)[5] visited Multan on the 10th April and stayed there till the evening of the 12th. All this time was occupied with conversations with Hindu and Mussulman representatives selected by their respective communities at public meetings held for the purpose. These conversations were first held separately with the representatives of each community and then with all of them jointly. At a previous joint meeting of some Hindus and Mohammedans the following six points were laid down for settlement :

Change of route of certain Tazia processions; the closing of certain beef and jhatka meet shops; boycott of Mohammedan labour by the Hindus; compensation to be paid by one community to the other; withdrawal of criminal cases pending against the members of both communities; Kucha Bandi.

It was stated that a common understanding was arrived at in respect of the last three points, and that the first three were left over for a subsequent meeting which never came off. The parties were not agreed as to the circumstances under which this attempt at a compromise failed and we dit not consider it necessary to investigate them. At the representative meeting held by us it was agreed that the six points enumerated above were the only points for disposal, but that the whole settlement hinged upon the first point, the others being only of secondary importance. We accordingly took up that point as the first and the main question at the express desire of the parties who conducted us along the route now in use and also that proposed for the future.

One of the objections taken by the Mussulmans to any change whatever was based on religious grounds but it was overruled by the only compotent authority among us (Maulana Azad) whose ruling was accepted on all hands. It appeared to us that a change of route, while putting Mohammedans to no serious inconvenience, afforded little or no guarantee against the recurrence of the trouble. On this being pointed out to the parties, the Hindu spokesman explained that his side being the more oppressed and aggrived party was insisting on a change more as a token of future goodwill of the Mohammedans than as an effective remedy for the evil, and with that object in view he suggested the following two alternatives.

The Mohammedans to pay compensation to the Hindus which had been officially estimated at Rs. 2,75,000 less Rs. 25,000 the estimated loss suffered by Mohammedans, or the closing of the slaughter houses and shops and stalls within the Municipal limits where beef was cooked and sold.

In the event of the inability of the Mohammedans to

accept either the proposed change of route or any of the two alternatives suggested, the Hindu spokesman invited them to make some offer to the Hindus which would have the desired effect and also to state if they had any demand to make from the Hindus which, he said, they were ready to entertain. The Mohammedan spokesman, however, expressed the inability of his community to accept any of the above proposals in its entirety but was willing to agree to the removal of the slaughter house from within the Municipal limits, provided the beef shops were maintained as at present. As to any demand of the Mussulmans against the Hindus, he stated, that they had none and added that the one consolation he could offer to the Hindus was to express his sincere regret for what had heppened. An impasse was thus reached and negotiations were broken off.

We then took occasion to address a mass meeting of Hindus and Mohammedans at which two of us (Maulana Azad and Pandit Motilal Nehru) explained at full length what had happened at the inter-communal conference and while advising the Mohammedans to see their way to accept any one of the proposals made by the Hindus, impresssd upon the latter the desirabality of forgetting the past without insisting upon any tests of future goodwill. We can only hope that the people will now take up the settlement of their differences in their own hands and dispense with their so-called representatives, who, we feel bound to say, did not approach the questions at issue in an unprejudiced and unselfish spirit.

Shuddhi and Sangathan

We all with the exception of Hakim Ajmal Khan[6] met Swami Shradhanand[7] and Kunwar Abdul Wahab Khan at Agra on the 5th of April and had an opportunity of conversing with a number of Malkana Rajputs. It is quite clear to us that the members of both communities are fully entitled to propagate their respective religions among these people and to induce them by peaceful persuasion to confine themselves to the religious practices of one community and give up those of the other. It is also open to the Malkanas to adopt such process of conversion or Shuddhi as they may be advised or be willing to undergo or to refuse to take part in any ceremony whatever. It is obvious that these undoubted rights can easily be exercised by individuals or groups of individuals following one religion without causing any insult, annoyance or injury to the members of other religions. We cannot too strongly condemn the use of force, coercion or undue influence and earnestly appeal to all the parties concerned to carry on only such propaganda as they may feel called upon to undertake by a compelling sense of religious duty and that in a friendly spirit strictly avoiding all that tends to create hostility between the sister communities.

It was reported to us that in certain villages where Malkana Rajputs had undergone Shuddhi in large numbers they had resorted to the very objectionable practice of harassing in various ways isolated men and women who had refused to go through the ceremony. Some cases of alleged cruelty and ill-treatment were mentioned to us while sitting together and other cases of a similar nature were brought to the notice of one of us (Maulana Azad). We regret we had no time to investigate any one of them on the spot in the presence of the parties concerned. But the fact that such complaints were made by Malkanas who were not well disposed to Shuddhi, shows that there is at least considerable apprehension of ill-treatment in their minds. The gentleman who had carried out most of the Shuddhi ceremonies admitted to us that he had heard of one or two cases of this kind but had taken no steps to verify the facts or adopt preventive measures. We take this opportunity to impress upon all the Shuddhi workers the imperative necessity of taking effective steps to see that the Malkanas who do not accept their teachings are not subjected to any hardship at the hands of those who have undergone Shuddhi or of any other person engaged in or about the propaganda.

The Hindu Sangathan is another movement allied to Shuddhi to which no exception can reasonably be taken if it is confined to the purpose which the name signalled, viz., the organization of Hindu society. Indeed both Hindu and Mussulman Sangathans are, in our opinion, eminently desirable to help the growth of the Indian Nation at the present stage of its existence. But such organizations have a way of degenerating into hostile communal associations and we have reason to suspect that the Hindu Sangathan is developing a tendency in that direction. The Mussulmans look upon it as a movement specially designed to harm them and have started a counter movement of a similar nature. There can be no doubt that the carrying on of these movements on wrong lines is calculated to intensify and perpetuate communal differences. We have taken occasion in our public speeches and private conversation with members of both movements who are men of light and leading will see to it that they are strictly confined and directed to the achievement of such reform in each community as is likely to be a source of strength to the other and to help in the onward march of both.

The Punjab Press

A reference to the files of the local newspapers revealed to us the regrettable fact that the highly coloured accounts of happenings in connection with Shuddhi and Sangathan movements given in the press of both communities and the strong language used in commenting upon them, had very largely contributed to inflame communal passions. We accordingly invited the editors of the newspapers published in Lahore to meet us in an informal conference to devise the best means of checking the mischief. We are glad to say that practically the whole Indian Press of Lahore willingly responded to our invitation and the informal conference held by us was converted then and there into a regular meeting of the press representatives which forthwith proceeded to form a Press Association and elect its committee and office-bearers. It was agreed that this Committee would in consultation with the Provincial Congress and Khilafat Committees take the necessary steps to verify all sensational communal news before publishing it and approach the consideration of all communal questions in a dignified and conciliatory tone. We hope that this Committee will fully justify our expectations and one of the most serious causes of communal differences would thereby be removed.

Communal Representation

We now come to the questions which are agitating the minds of the educated classes in the Punjab.

We are told that according to the Mussulman demand seats in the Councils, in the Municipalities and District Boards, in the University and also public offices should be divided amongst different communities according to their numerical strength and unless that was done there could be no peace in the Punjab. The Hindus and the Sikhs, on the other hand, were against communal representation of any kind. With a view to see whether a via media could be found we invited certain Hindus and Mussulmans of this province who represent extreme views on both sides to elect two representative committees. This Committee was subsequently enlarged by the addition of one representative of the Hindu Sabha and another of the Muslim League and the presidents of the Provincial Congress and Khilafat Committees and also of the Shiromani Gurdwara Parbandhak Committee. These Committees met for the purpose and after a good deal of discussion a smaller Committee was elected consisting of ourselves and two representatives from each of the three communities. This representative Committee met on several days, discussed all possible questions with reference to these disputes, but unfortunately could not arrive at any concluded agreement. The various suggestions and counter suggestions made lead us to the belief that had the proposal of dividing the seats in the Council in the proportion of 45, 30 and 25 per cent amongst the Mohammedans, the Hindus and (the) Sikhs respectively been accepted by the Mohammedans, the other communities would have agreed to the same proportion in the Municipalities and in the District Boards with separate communal electorates and that it would have been possible to arrive at some arrangement where Hindus and Mohammedans could be assured of alternately representing the University. But the Mohammedans who formed nearly 56 per cent of population and were allowed only 50 per cent representation under the Lucknow Pact did not agree to a further reduction which would have the effect of converting their majority into a minority as against a possible combine of non-Muslim representatives. Communal representation is admittedly an evil from the national point of view but we think that in the existing circumstances and until greater national solidarity is attained, the system, though wrong in principle, should be accepted by all the parties concerned and that the three communities should join hands in pressing upon the Government a demand for a very extensive franchise and for the abolition of official seats on the Council, the Municipal and District Board and in the University. After a satisfactory settlement in respect of communal representation in the elective bodies is reached, the three communities should, without the help of any legislation to that effect, agree to have a reasonable proportion in the Government and Municipal offices. It is however necessary to point out that this result should be attained gradually by filling up posts in the different departments, keeping in view the proportion agreed upon without superseding present incumbents or applying any such obviously unjust method.

As we have already said these disputes are confined to a very limited number of the educated population who always place their own selfish interests above the interests of the nation as a whole. But in view of the fact that it is impossible to prevent this class of people from exploiting the masses, we feel that peace in the Punjab depends in a greater measure on a satisfactory solution of their demands. So far as the bulk of the population is concerned, they are very little troubled by the disputes we have mentioned.

Other Matters

As no formal settlement could be arrived at on the question of communal representation the other points, raised by the parties in their respective notes of communal grievances, were not formally dealt with but certain principles were generally agreed upon in the course of discussion. These were put in the form of resolutions by the president (Mr. C.R. Das)[8] and copies were supplied to the members of the joint committee. We give below the draft resolutions as showing the general trend of opinion in the Punjab and the reasonable frame of mind in which we found all parties concerned on the questions involved.

Draft Resolutions

That to remove all misundertakings, doubts and suspicions regarding the connection of the Mohammedans with what is called Pan-Islamic activities, this Committee declares that although it is right and natural for Indian Mohammedans to sympathise with Mohammedans in other parts of the world and to take necessary steps to vindicate the rights of the Khilafat, there is no reason for any apprehension that they would join any Mohammedan invader of India and that on the contrary it is the duty of every true Mohammedan no join the Hindus and others in expelling any such invasion.

That this committee further points out that expression of opinion regarding this matter by individual Hindus or Mussulmans, which in any way contradicts the above mentloned declaration, should be taken as the outcome of undue and unworthy suspicion and should not be made the foundation of an attack on either community.

That this Committee further resolves that it should be constantly borne in mind by all communities in the Punjab that India is open for any community or communities but that India is for the Indians and stands for the fusion or federation of all communities.

That whereas each community has the right of converting others to its faith, no unfair means should be used and no oppression should be resorted to and where any such case is alleged it should be investigated by the Punjab Reconciliation Board to be appointed by this Committee and the decision of the said Board should be accepted by the eommunities concerned. (The namcs of some leading gentlemen were noted as members of the Board).

That inasmuch as the local press has undortunately contributed to much of the ill-feeling between the different communities, the said Board should meet the Editors and Managers of Indian newspapers and take such steps with their concurrence as may prevent such misthief and should in particular request them not to publish any cases of communal injustice or oppression before the same have been investigated by the Reconciliation Board. (Necessary steps in the connection have already been taken).

That whereas the preservation of cows and the prevention of their slaughter is considered desirable by all communities on economic grounds and whereas there is a large body of Mohammedan opinion in favour of voluntary prevention of cow slaughter in difference to the Hindus feeling in respect thereof, this Committee resolves that no Hindu or Hindus should propose or cause to be proposed any legislation regarding cow killing without the concurrence of the Mohammedan community and further that any dispute or difference in respect of cow slaughter or prevention thereof, should be referred to and decided by the Reconciliation Board.

That the Committee further resolves that any attempt by any one community to boycott any other community socially or economically or in any other way is foolish, unjust and unworthy of both communities and that any dispute or difference arising by reason of such an attempt should also be settled by the said Board whose decision must be accepted by the parties coneerned in both dispute or difference.

That the Committee recommends that the three communities in the Punjab should enter into national pact regarding the Council and the Municipal and other local Boards full particulars of which are set out in the schedule which is to be taken as a part of this resolution and it is resolved that any disputes and differences which may arise from non-observance thereof should be settled and adjusted by the said Board. (As the negotiations were broken up no schedule was prepared).

C.R. Das, Abul Kalam Azad,
Sarojini Naidu, Ajmal Khan, Motilal Nehru.

(66)

Joint[1] Statement by Maulana Azad and Motilal Nehru on the Hindu-Muslim dispute at Nagpur[2] 13th Junuary, 1925.

In October last leading Hindus and Musalmans of Nagpur agreed to be bound by our decision on the question whether there was any and if so what custom prevalent in the city of Nagpur from of old relating to the playing of processional music in front or in the vicinity of mosques at all or any specified times of the day and night. This reference involved the taking of evidence for which we were then unable to spare the necessary time. We came back to Nagpur on the 11th January and on the following day held a sitting with a view to go into the question, We had a most pleasant surprise in store for us. At the commencement of the proceedings it was stated on behalf of the Musalmans that while they fully believed that there was a custom to stop all music when passing their mosques they had after full consideration of the matter and in the interests of an abiding unity between the two communitics determined to surrender their legal right and to leave it to the good sense of the Hindus to play or stop music as they thought fit. They made it clear that although the playing of music in front of mosques while they were at congregational prayers was most annoying to them they have made up their minds to suffer such annoyance rather than proceed with an enquiry on the merits of the question which in any event was bound to leave unpleasantness behind and retard a speedy resoteation of amicable relations. We congratulate the Musalmans on their wise and patriotic determination and thank them for having relieved us of the painful duty of deciding a controversy between the sister communitics which had caused considerable bitterness. We asked the Musalmans to give us in writing the substance of their generous offer and close the formal proceedings reserving to the Hindus liberty to submit any statement they might be advised to make in response to the Musalman offer. Both parties filed written statements in the course of the day. The Musalman statement repeated the offer we have set out above.

The Hindus expressed their full appreciation of the spirit in which the Musalmans had withdrawn their objection to the playing of music in front of mosques and undertook to see that the Musalmans were put to the least inconvenience consistently with the due discharge of what the Hindus considered to be their religious duty. They reserved liberty to play music along public streets and thorough fares at all times of the day and night only when such music accompanied what they described as the traditional annual processions of the royal family of the Bhonslas and the traditional Jajoba procession. In regard to all other processions they offered to stop music when passing five specified mosques named below between the hours of one and one thirty p.m. and five and five thirty p.m. in the months of October to February and six and six thirty p.m. in the remaining months of the year. It will appear from the above statements that the Musalmans of Nagpur have fully complied with the resolution passed on the subject by the Unity Conference at Delhi[3] in withdrawing their objections and leaving it to the good sense of the Hindus to avoid causing them any inconvenience. This resolution was passed after full and matured consideration by representative Hindus and Musalamans and affords a clear guidance to both communities as to the duty each owes to the other. In the last clause of the resolution the Hindu members of the Conference call upon their co-religionists to refrain from playing music in front of mosques in such a way as to cause any disturbance to Muhamedans at the times of their congregational prayers.

The Hindus of Nagpur felt themselves compelled by their religious obligations to limit their offer of stopping music to five mosques only and that at the time of only two out of five daily congregational prayers. Various reasons more or less of a local character were assigned for this limitation but in view of the unconditional offer of the Musalmans we thought it unnecessary to enquire further into the matter. We, therefore express no opinion as to the soundness or otherwise of these reasons. It is, however, obvious that no discrimination can be made between one mosque or another or between one prayer and another in regard to playing of music.

We hope and trust that in the absence of any question of

custom the special case of Nagpur will not only be not treated as a precedent for such discrimination in other parts of India but that the Nagpur Hindus themselves will do away with it in course of time. We have reason to believe that the friendly relations which have now been restored will in due course acquire sufficient strength to render all distinction and discrimination unnecessary. We note with pleasure that the Musalamans declared their full adherence to their offer after they came to know of the terms of the Hindu undertaking and that Dr. Moonje, as President of the public meeting addressed by us, assured the Musalmans on behalf of the Hindus of Nagpur that the brotherly feelings of the former would be fully reciprocated by the latter.

We congratulate both parties and also the Hindus and Muslamans of India in general at the happy settlement arrived at.

Motilal Nehru
A.K. Azad

(67)

The[1] Nehru-AzadManifesto.[2] **31st July, 1926**

"Dear Sir,—you have no doubt realised the evident danger of the new phase into which the communal movements in India are now entering. The situation is going daily from bad to worse and we feel that if no immediate organised effort is made, this rising tide will soon overwhelm the whole field of our political and civic life. You will perhaps agree with us that in the main, our present troubles are due to the fact that by an indiscriminate mixing up of the politieal and religious issues, we have initiated a revivalist section which, because of the existence of heterogenous elements in our country, makes a cultural and social conflict inevitable and it is clear that the only real remedy which can save us from disaster is the deliberate establishment in our midst of a national consciousness and a national atmosphere in which religious and communal conflicts and passions will be relegated to a subordinate and a lower plane.

A Non-Communal Association Essential

"But the question which is troubling the best Indian minds to-day is how to achieve this object effectively. The attitude of general inaction and of passive disapproval which has so far been maintained, is an index not so much of our indifference to the dangers of the situation as of the complex and delicate nature of the problems involved and of the tremendous difficulties which have to be faced before reaching the resolution. Further inaction will, however, only multiply these difficulties and make it impossible to grapple with them even with such chance of success as we have at present. The new trend of the Hindu Maha Sabha movement on the one side and of the Muslim communal movements on the other threaten a crisis which makes some positive action imperative on the part of those who yet happen to retain their balance. Accordingly, we have decided to start a movement to rally to a centre and organise those sections of enlightened Indians who agree with us that communalism is a negation of nationalism and that continued communal conflicts from our national life must be preceded by suitable steps to organise our civic life in such a way as to make violent communal outbursets difficult, if not impossible and to establish points of contact between the two communities to prepare a way for the adjustment of mutual differences. You will agree that by far the largest sections of the Hindus and the Musalmans in India want to live together in peace, if not in unity. The peasants, the industrial classes and the wealthy are sure to welcome any movement for peace and unity and be ready to co-operate in the materialisation of its aims. Among the educated classes, the major portion would willingly help freeing civic life from the constant dreads and evident dangers of violent communal outbursts. If, therefore, a movement for unity and peace is launched, it is bound to receive a ready and generous response from the people. On the contrary, if even at this stage, organised effort is not made in this direction, all these various sections would gradually drift towards communalism and ultimately get involved in struggle. It is time that we should make a determined effort to rally and organise these sections and, in this way, isolate, weaken and discredit these mischievous elements in our society which are really responsible for the present crisis. A movement of this nature can be effectively carried on only by an highly organised body of men of all communities who are themselves absolutely free from communal bias of any kind, and are united together by a common bond of fellowship in the struggle against communalism. For the purpose of bringing together such a body of men, it is necessary to arrive at a clear understanding of certain principles which are to guide them in their relations to each other and the public at large. We are thus inevitably led to think of organising a new association or party. Our proposal may, at first sight, appear to be only an attempt to add one more to the numerous parties that came into being with the avowed object of evolving order out of chaos but only succeeded in making confusion worse confounded. But a little reflection will show that we are scrupulously eliminating the one element which, as experience has shown, was solely responsible for the failure of these parties, viz., their purely communal basis. We claim no originality that ours is the first serious endeavour to carry out the idea in practice. We are, therefore, approaching friends whom we believe to be above all communal prejudice to invite their help and co-operation in this important undertaking. Generally speaking, the following may be taken as the guiding principles we have referred to above : (a) full liberty of religious view and practices; (b) absolute tolerance of the views and practices of others; (c) adjustment of communal relations on the basis of strict legal rights of communities and individuals.

Proposed Indian National Union[3]

"We propose that the new organisation be called the Indian National Union. The immediate object will be to avoid communal conflicts in their present forms. The end ultimately in view will be to bring about a thorough understanding between the different communities on a solid and permanent basis. All Indians of whatever community who subscribe to the above principles, will be welcomed as members of the Union, provided they do not belong to any communal organisation. It is evident that the inclusion of those who belong to a movement, which seeks to enforce the rights of only one community against another, would defeat our whole purpose. We fully expect that the success of the national movement we are trying to start will, in due course, attract many members of the existing communal organisations and that they will find no difficulty in joining us by retiring from the latter. It is highly desirable that the proposed organisation should be truly national and wholly non-political and that except for the bar on members of communal organisations, no party shall be excluded so as to make it possible for all shades of political thought to join. It will be noticed that all of those who have agreed to join the proposed union, do not hold identical views on political questions. We have considered it necessary to make this point quite clear at the very start. The general attitude of such a party towards the various communities or towards those that may arise hereafter, will have to be determincd exclusively by reason and justice, as our main object will be a persistent propaganda against all forms of communalism. The details of these and other cognate matters can only be settled at the preliminary meeting of the Union and it is unnecessary to deal with them at this stage.

Mixed Boards to Settle Disputes

It may, however, be noted that the old idea of establishing mixed boards for the settlement of mutual disputes has never so far been given a fair trial and it is time that serious effort was made to try this experiment on an extensive basis. We can gradually train panchayats to act equitably in the discharge of their duties and it may be possible to take the principles incorporated in the resolutions of the Unity Conference at Delhi as a basis.

A Proposed Preliminary Meeting

"We are fully alive to the difficulties of carrying out the

programme which we are putting before you but we are doing so with the conviction that there is no lack of men and women in the country entirely free from communal bias who will only be too glad to help in overcoming all obstacles. We hope you will give to the matter the attention it deserves and will send your considered opinion at your early convenience. We propose to call a meeting of those who intimate their approval of our suggestions on an early date at some convenient centre, with the object of formally inaugurating the movement, the framing of the necessary rules and the election of office bearers. Meanwhile, the undersigned will act as a provisional committee and appoint a provisional Secretary. It is requested that all replies be addressed to the latter at Anand Bhavan, Allahabad".

(68)

Maulana[1] Azad and Dr. Ansari's Appeal[2]. 2nd January, 1930.

"We have no doubt in our mind that Musalmans owe it to their motherland to respond to the historic call of the Congress and join it with cheerful determination to see the national struggle through".

(69)

Joint[1] Appeal by Maulana Azad and other Congress Leaders on the Riots in Kanpur. (March, 1931).

We the undersigned deeply deplore the terrible tragedy of Cawnpore[2] resulting in a large number of deaths including the death of Syt. Ganesh Shankar Vidyarthi[3], one of the noblest of workers who was trying to rescue those who were in danger. All accounts go to show that this true servant of the nation was a true nationalist free from any communal taint and respected equally by both the parties. We ask all lovers of peace to work in their respective areas so as to remove every cause of distrust or suspicion and seek occasions for both the communities to meet together and promote the common good.

We are convinced that there are more points of contact and common interest between us the infinitely less of differences. Chief among the former is the economic life which is impossible to be led in isolation. Common birth makes us inter-dependent in daily life. It is easy enough to see that both must perish if each lived its daily life apart from the other. He, therefore, who parts the two and sets one community against the other is the enemy of his own and must be treated as such.

At this juncture we cannot lay too much stress upon the necessity of not magnifying every petty quarrel into a communal grievance and using it as a signal for strife. On such occasions a Hindu should make it a point of honour to run to the rescue of his Mussalman brother and a Mussalman in similar circumstances to his Hindu brother and thus by mutual help lay the foundation for a true unity.

(70)

Azad-Nehru[1] Statement[2] **(September, 1939)**

We have read the Viceroy's statement with deep regret. If this is the final answer of the British Government to the people of India, then, there is no common ground between the two and our path diverge completely.

The whole statement is a complete repudiation of all that India stands for nationally and internationally. It is a statement which would have been out of date twenty years ago; today it has absolutely no relation to reality. There is no mention in it of independence, freedom, democracy or self-determination; no attempt even to justify the dragooning of India into the war without reference to her being forced to join an advance for objectives which are not her's. These objectives appear clearly from the Viceroy's statement to be the preservation and maintenance of the British imperial and financial structure in India and abroad.

The "better international system", to which the British Premier has referred, is evidently meant to preserve and strengthen this structure. Apart from this, it relates, according to him, to the peoples of Europe and not to Asia or

Africa. India continues where she is; the colonies remain where they are; imperialism is still meant to flourish.

All this seems to follow from the Viceroy's statement and if this is the aim of the war it is difficult to imagine that even the British Government living as it does in an age that is past and done with, can expect any self-respecting Indian to co-operate with it.

The hand of friedship the Congress had extended to the British people in this hour of world crisis has been spurned by their Government. How far that Government represents them, it is for them to say, but we have to consider the Viceroy's statement as England's reply to India.

What our next steps should be it would be premature and improper for us to say at this stage. That is for the Working Committee to decide and the Committee is meeting for that purpose soon. The hour is a grave one and requires all our united wisdom and courage and discipline and mutual forbearance. Let us bear ourselves with dignity and restraint and hold together in the cause of India's freedom.

(71)

Statement[1] by Maulana Azad[2] (November, 1939)

I have read the Viceroy's statement published alongwith the correspondence that passed between him and Mr. Jinnah and myself. He seems to give an impression that the British Government are unable to comply with our request for a clear declaration of India's status as a free country on account of our differences. The fact is that the British Government is not prepared to promise that it will accept and give legal effect to any constitution which the Indians, including all real minorities, would prepare and in which the safeguards for the protection of minorities will be included. We made a public demand for such a promise and I cannot understand what objections the British Government can have to this on the score of our differences with the minorities. If we are unable to produce a constitution satisfactory to all, the British

Government will be free from all blame and the responsibility will be entirely of the Indians. The minorities which are really for attaining the freedom of India can have no reasonable objection as the proposed constitution will not be produced without cooperation of all.

The real difficulty is not communal but political. The British Government are not yet prepared to concede the right of self-determination to India in practice, however, much it may proclaim it in theory to the world. We put its professions to acid test. Let us have a right to frame our own constitution and we shall do it. We failed in the past in assisting the British Government to frame a constitution for us. But helping the British Government to frame a constitution for India is something very different from independently framing a constitution for ourselves with certainty that the constitution will be accepted and enforced.

Our regret it that instead of adopting this straight course and throwing the responsibility upon the Indians to frame a constitution with necessary and satisfactory safeguards for the protection of the minorities and thus showing its own bonafides beyond doubt and cavil, the British Government befogged the main and moral issue by asking us to settle our differences without telling us at the same time that the result of such a settlement will be a free constitution for the country. It was for this reason that we felt compelled to concentrate on political issues and to refuse to consider the proposal for the expansion of the viceroy's Executive Council before the question of India's status as a free country with full right to self-determination is settled to our satisfaction.

The two principal organisations of which the Viceroy made reference in his statement, the Indian National Congress and the All-India Muslim League both declared that they aim at the independence for India and so far as I know there is no party or group in India which does not want full powers for India to manage her own affairs by whatever name or expression that freedom may be called or described. There is this fundamental unity in all parties in India and this is a universal urge of all Indians which the Congress embodied in its demand for a clear declaration.

The resolution of the Muslim League is equally clear that it does not accept the Viceroy's announcement and insists upon the clarification of the same and consideration *de novo* of the question of Indian constitution. How then does any communal difference stand in the way of clear recognition and declaration of the status as a free country ? Whatever differences there are relate not to India but to certain other subsidiary matters which we are prepared to settle ourselves. Our proposed talks with Mr. Jinnah[3] will relate not to this fundamental position, but other subsidiary matters. The Congress has been insisting on, "constructive programme an essential element of which" as Mr. Jinnah recognises "is communal unity". We propose to do our best to achieve the success of this essential programme, but the fact that we are still engaged in this most urgent work should not stand in the way of a clear declaration of the kind demanded by us. All points of principle and detail for safeguarding the rights of the minorities have to be left out to be settled by Indians themselves which they will do to the satisfaction of all if once the British Government proves its own bonafides by ceasing to meddle in our domestic affairs.

(72)

Maulana[1] Azad's Statement[2] (April, 1940)

The General Secretary of the All India Congress Committee has drawn the attention of the Congress organisations towards the approach of the National Week and reminded them of their tasks. I am confident that on this occasion all Congress Committees will fully demonstrate their capacity for action. In this connection I expect of every Congressman and woman, every supporter of the Congress cause to contribute in a practical manner towards the success of the week.

For the last 20 years this week has come to stay as the season of our constructive efforts. Like the natural seasons of our land, this one also recurs every year, and after influencing us for a while, passes on. Our natural seasons affect us physically, while this one reacts on our intellect and emotions. It provides us with a rare opportunity for self-introspection and self-purification in order that we examine afresh our hearts and our minds. It comes to gauge how far our professions of service, sacrifice and non-violence which we repeat so often, have penetrated into the depths of our hearts. For us this year the approach of the National Week has a special significance.

Only a few days back we have announced to the world from the Congress platform at Ramgarh, our new passion for freedom and our determination to achieve it. The National Week is thus the first stage of testing the value of these announcements. If, at this stage, we live up to the true ideal of our constructive programme it would provide us with those inner resources without which it would be difficult for us to acquaint ourselves with honour in the coming struggle.

How then do we expect to fulfil the requirements of the constructive programme? The constructive programme implies Hindu-Muslim unity, removal of untouchability and extensive popularisation of Khadi. Do we imagine that by holding a few meetings and delivering speeches, we would fulfil the task assigned for the National Week? Does it suffice, for us that we go about hawking Khadi for a week in the streets and bye-lanes of the towns and then come back to our normal occupations with the feeling that we have done our duty to the constructive programme?

Of course, all these, are necessary items of the programme, and we must carry them out. But this alone would not do. These activities undoubtedly give shape and form to our efforts but we require something more to put life into it. We Congressmen profess to shoulder the great burden of our national movement in India today and ours undoubtedly is the responsibility in every phase of thought and action. If we imbibe the true spirit of the constructive programme, I have no hesitation in affirming that every atom of this land will respond to the call of national life.

But do we expect to carry warmth to others if our own hearths grow cold? No, we must kindle our own fires first. The National Week provides us with that opportunity.

(73)

Maulana[1] Azad's Statement **22nd April, 1940**

Maulana Abul Kalam Azad, the Congress President, issued a statement on Lord Zetland's[2] speech in the House of Lords on the situation in India, "Lord Zetland's speech leaves things where they have been since the breakdown of the negotiations between Lord Linlithgrow and Mr. Gandhi in February. I can only say that every difficulty that the Secretary of State raises is completely met by the proposed constituent assembly. The issue is simple. Is the British Government prepared to admit the right of self-administration for India ? If she is, then there can be only one proper method of finally deciding all the problems, that is, they should be referred to the elected representatives of India. Only such an assembly can deal with problems relating to Hindus and Moslems and the Indian States."

(74)

Maulana[1] Azad's Statement on Waziristan[2] **7th July, 1940**

The Congress Working Committee have given frequent and earnest thought to the problem of raiding on the Frontier. They were distressed by this because of the suffering and insecurity it caused and also because it led to bitterness and ill-will between our people and our neighbours across the Frontier. They realised, however, that the way to solve this problem was to approach the Border Tribes in a friendly way. They advised Khan Abdul Gaffar Khan and his colleagues of the Frontier Province to seek contacts with the Waziris by sending a deputation to Waziristan but unfortunately the Government refused to give permission for this deputation.

The Working Committee have again considered the grave situation that exists and conferred with Khan Abdul Gaffar Khan. They have decided to depute two of their members, Mr. Bholabhai Desai and Mr. Asaf Ali, to proceed to the Frontier, to develop contacts with the Waziris and other Border tribes and to study the problem in all its aspects. I am sure that their visit will prove of help to us in dealing with this problem. I trust that the Government will give every facility to these two representatives of ours.

It has long been our declared policy and desire to have friendly relations with our neighbour nations and peoples and we are convinced that when we have the chance, we shall be able to do so with advantage to all concerned. A free India will be strong enough to protect her frontiers but the real strength that we seek to build is the friendship of our Border peoples. We shall try to understand their difficulties and make them understand ours and the contacts that we shall develop will, we trust, bring peace and security and economic betterment to both sides of the Frontiers.

(75)

Maulana[1] Azad's Statement[2] **27th July, 1940**

It was hardly four months and two weeks since they (we) met at Ramgarh but during this short period the world had changed almost out of recognition. This change was not only in respect of outward form but it had almost brought about a revolution in ideas and beliefs. It would not be possible for us not to be affected by all that has happened and, therefore, it becomes our duty to review our own position and take stock of the situation with a view to seeking what changes we should make in our own attitude.

Two important decisions of the Congress Working Committee are to be placed before you. One of these is known as the Wardha Statement. Although there is nothing new in it, as it relates to the basic policy of the Indian National Congress, it becomes our duty to consider it as this House represents the Congress.

It was not at the Wardha meeting in June last that Mahatma Gandhi raised the question of non-violence for the first time. He had raised it two years ago. In September 1938 the All India Congress Committee met at Delhi. At this meeting of the Congress Working Committee Mahatma Gandhi raised the issue of extending the principle of non-violence which the Congress had followed in regard to its internal policy for the last twenty years to other spheres.

Mahatma Gandhi wanted the Congress at this stage to declare that a free India would eschew all violence and would have no army to defend the country against aggression. The Congress should thus depend entirely upon non-violence for the purpose of dealing with internal disorders and external aggression. Mahatma Gandhi felt that he had to give the message of non-violence to the world and if he could not persuade his own countrymen to accept it, it would be difficult for him to preach it to others. The Congress Working Committee felt itself unable to accept his position and explained its difficulties to Mahatma Gandhi. The issue, however, did not assume any serious proportion then as the Munich Agreement postponed the war.

The question was again raised by Mahatma Gandhi when war broke out in September last. In November last when Gandhiji went to interview the Viceroy he asked me and other members of the Working Committee to relieve him of the responsibility of guiding the Congress policy and leave him free to pursue in his own way, the policy of non-violence. The Committee, however, once again persuaded Mahatma Gandhi to postpone decision. At Ramgarh Mahatma Gandhi raised this question for the third time. On this occasion Mahatma Gandhi also referred to other weakness in the Congress organisation and expressed a desire to be relieved of responsibility. This came as a shock to the Working Committee and if I had not practically forced Mahatma Gandhi to postpone decision of the issue once again, a crisis would have arisen as early as at Ramgarh.

You will thus see that this issue had been hanging fire for over two years and when we meet in Wardha in June last Mahatma Gandhi wanted the Committee to make up its mind once for all, as the international situation had become deticate and he felt that a decision on such a vital issue could not be postponed any longer. Even then I tried to persuade Mahatma Gandhi once again to postpone the matter as I knew the dangers and the difficulties of a decision, There is not a soul in the Congress who is not anxious to go the whole length with Mahatma Gandhim if he can help it; but we cannot close our eyes to hard facts. We know that arms and ammunitions have not been able to save the freedom of France, Holland, Belgium and Norway but we also know that human nature, even after realising the futility of armed resistance, is not prepared to give up force. We had not the courage to declare that we shall organise a State in this country without an armed force. If we did, it would be wrong on our part. Mahatma Gandhi has to give the message of non-violence to the world and, therefore, it is his duty to propagate it but we have to consider our position as the representatives of the Indian Nation meeting in the Indian National Congress. The Indian National Congress is a political organisation pledged to win the political independence of the country. It is not an institution for organising world peace.

Honestly we cannot go as far as Mahatma Gandhi wants us to go. We admit that it is a weakness on our part but it is a weakness which we share with the entire humanity. Though we cannot go with Mahatma Gandhi the whole hog, we do not wish to stop him from pursuing his own path. Yet realising the loss that the Congress would suffer on being deprived of Mahatma Gandhi's guidance, I was tempted to approach him once again to defer his decision on this issue. I had thrice succeeded in my attempt but this time, I failed because Mahatma Gandhi pointed out that it was no use postponing his decision on this vital issue for the moment was fast approaching when the Congress would have to take a final decision and therefore, it was better that each party decided to follow its own path. I placed the whole matter before the Working Committee and invited separately the opinion of each member. Most of us felt that we were not able to take up the grave responsibility of declaring that we would completely eschew violence when we had to deal with widespread internal disorder in this country or external aggression. But we all were quite clear in our minds that so far as the struggle for winning our independence was concerned non-violence would continue to occupy the same place in the Congress programme that it had occupied all these 20 years. We all felt that the slightest deviation in this respect will mean political suicide for the Congress.

Whatever success we have achieved in our struggle during all these years has been due to our unflinching faith in non-violence and if we have not succeeded to the extent to which we ought to have succeeded, it is due to our inability to practice non-violence to the fuller extent. If we ever give up this idea, we shall be burying the Congress. I feel I must take you further in confidence and inform you that there are four members of the Working Committee, Babu Rajendra Prasad, Dr. Prafulla Chandra Ghose, Mr. Kripalani and Mr. Shankerrao Deo who feel that they can go the whole length with Mahatma Gandhi. You already know about Khan Abdul Ghaffar Khan.

There are people who think that by passing the Delhi Resolution the Congress Working Committee has made a departure from past resolutions. I wish to emphasise that this is a wrong view. Even if we wished to take a new step we could not do so because we have behind us a series of resolutions and statements issued from time to time by the Congress Working Committee during the past few months. We cannot domolish all these. We have not the right to do so. We have not the power to do so. Changes in the international situation, however, are so serious that we cannot shut our eyes to them and proceed blindly. We have not abated our original demand in any way. We have demanded the unequivocal declaration of India's independence. As a provisional measure we have asked for the establishment of a representative national government.

Although Mahatma Gandhi would not be responsible for the policy of the Congress any longer, his advice would always be available to the Working Committee and the Congress. Our relations will continue with him as long as he lives and I pray to God, that he may be spared long to guide us. We must, however, realise that the nature of his guidance will not be the same as before and this adds greatly to our responsibility. We have a great objective to achieve; we have an ideal before us which is sufficient to inspire any group of peopie. There may be ups and downs and difficulties may beset our path but we need not be disheartened or dis-spirited by these.

We have to solve every difficulty that presents itself to us and we have also to recognise the hard fact of Mahatma Gandhi's separation from us. We must bear it bravely. In this difficult hour, it is our duty to be united. I, therefore, appeal to you to sink all differences and to face bravely the trials that lie ahead of us. This is what the country demands from us and this is what the Congress expects us to do. If we fail in this hour of trial, the world will have a poor opinion of us; but I am sure that we shall not fail.

(76)

Maulana[1] Azad's statement on Burma-China Road[2] (July, 1940)

The decision of the British Government to close the Burma-China Road is a matter of the most serious significance for China, India, Burma and Britain. This road had been built at enormous sacrifice by China and already it had become one of the main arteries of traffic between China and the outer world. It had brought China and Burma and India nearer to one another and their contacts grew from day to day. The people of India welcome this new relationship and their goodwill flowed out to the people of China struggling for their freedom against an aggressor nation. The closing of the Burma road means a severe restriction on these growing contacts and a flouting of Indian opinion. It is in complete conflict with the foreign policy which the people of India desire to pursue. It is a violation of international usage as well as of Sino-British treaties and is evidently meant to hamper China in her struggle for freedom. It is clearly an encouragement of the aggressor nation who for over three years has been carrying on an undeclared war on Chinese territory. It is support of a policy against which Great Britain claims to be fighting in Europe. Its greatest significance lies in the light it throws on British policy which claims to do one thing in Europe and follows an entirely different course in India and China. We must, therefore, wholly disapprove of the action of the British Government in closing the Burma-China Road.

(77)

Maulana[1] Azad's Press Interview[2] **(October, 1940)**

"I admit that the outcome of the Simla meeting is not contrary to expectations." The Congress President added, "The very presence of the British Government in India indicates one reality from whatever angle we see the denial of free will of India. Naturally, therefore, we cannot expect her to tolerate the free expression of our decision about the war, even if it be of a purely non-violent nature".

(78)

Maulana[1] Azad's Statement[2] **(22nd March, 1942)**

The Maulana said that India should take a lesson from the experience of various European countries. India was no longer a spectator; the time for her trial had arrived. The question of the future of Muslims in India was a vital questiou and it had been worrying him for the last thirty-eight years. During this period, there had been no change in his attitude towards this question. He had been trying to find out the root cause and had come to the conclusion that, unless they were free from British imperialism, no other question should be raised. Muslims should not ask for any safeguards but should try to attain the country's freedom first. He was confident that no earthly power could efface nine crores of Muslims in this country. Nor any constitution or safeguards could save them if they had no confidence in themselves and did not attempt to stand on their owe legs.

(79)

Maulana[1] Azad at a Press Conference[2] **(10th April, 1942)**

Maulana Abul Kalam Azad met a large number of journalists on April 11th in Delhi and spoke to them about his talks with Sir Stafford Cripps. In particular, he referred to his first interview with Sir Stafford and said that he laid emphasis on these issues:

Firstly, I told Sir Stafford that the approach to the Indian problem made in the Draft Declaration was not only not correct but was likely to lead to greater complications. If the British Government desired to infuse a new spirit in India even at this eleventh hour and send out a person like Sir Stafford for the task, the simple method would have been to send out through Sir Stafford the announcement that Britain was prepared to part with power. Sir Stafford could then have asked Indians to draw up a scheme. If we failed to draw one up, the entire responsibility would have been ours.

Sir Stafford, in reply, referred to the first part of the Draft Declaration and asserted that it was a considered decision of principle. He added that provision had already been made in it for different political organisations and it was open to them to come to an agreement at any time.

"I pointed out", said the Maulana, "that after concrete proposals had been introduced by him, the task of independent agreement among the parties in India had been made difficult".

"Secondly", proceeded the Maulana, "I told Sir Stafford that the Draft Declaration laid much greater emphasis on the future than on the immediate present while India demanded changes in the present system. The proposals relating to the present were not positive; they were negative.

"I said to him that as far as the Congress was concerned I do not see how it could accept the proposals. War, I said, was threatening India; but the light had gone out of the hearts of the millions who might have sacrificed themselves for their country.

"Our common task now demanded that we should find a psychological approach in order to re-kindle the spark of patriotic fervour in those hearts. This could not be achieved merely by holding out promises for the future but people must be made to feel that they were free in their own country to-day and had to defend their own freedom and their own country.

"Sir Stafford, speaking with great confidence, assured me that clause (e) of the Draft Declaration provided for complete freedom and transfer of power, with only one reservation about defence.

"I then pointed out that defence of the country was the demand of the moment as far as the country was concerned and during the war civil administration had disappeared because problems of defence permeated every civil department, and if you reserved defence you practically reserve all the powers which you say are being transferred to India.

"Sir Stafford said by way of reassurance that the reservations related only to the functions of the Commander-in-Chief.

"The rest of the discussion proceeded in respect of this particular question.

"The third point emphasised by me was that in tackling the political question in India, communal questions were bound to arise at some stage or other and would have to be solved. I assured him that as soon as the main political problem was settled, the responsibility of finding a satisfactory solution of the communal and other problems would be ours, and I could confidently assert that we would find a satisfactory solution.

"Sir Stafford entirely agreed with me and said this was exactly what he had said before the War Cabinet before he came out to India.

"This naturally conjured up in my mind a picture of the present not found in the cold words of the Draft Declaration, and I, therefore, naturally decided to call a meeting of the Working Committee to examine it.

"I, however, regret to say that the first impression of the picture created as a result of my earlier interviews with Sir Stafford gradually became blurred as the discussions on material points proceeded from stage to stage. And when I last met him on the night of April 9, the whole picture had completely faded out."

Referring to his interview with General Wavell,[3] the Maulana said : "In the course of our talks, Sir Stafford Cripps had repeatedly emphasised the technical difficulties in the way of transferring defence to an Indian member. He had suggested that we should meet General Wavell, because he could explain the technical side of the question much better.

"But curiously enough, throughout our interview with the Commander-in-Chief, at which other military officers were present not a word was spoken about any technical difficulty;

the entire discussion proceeded on political lines. It did not strike me for a moment that we were interviewing a military expert but an expert politician.

"I think," the Maulana went on, "I must clarify the position created by certain speculations in a section of the press as regards Mahatma Gandhi's part in the discussions. The Mahatma's views as regards participation in any war are well known and it would be entirely untrue to suggest that the Working Committee's decisions have in any way been influenced by those views.

"In fact, Mahatma Gandhi made it clear to the Working Committee that they were perfectly free to come to their own decisions on the merits of the proposals. He did not really want to participate even in the earlier sittings of the Working Committee but he was persuaded by me to stay on from day to day as long as he could afford to do so. Eventually, my persuasion proved powerless to make him stay longer.

"I want to repeat what I said yesterday that the Working Committee's decision has at every stage been unanimous," he declared.

"He concluded: "It is deeply to be regretted that the aim which all of us had passionately desired has not been reached but I must acknowledge that all these discussions were carried on in a friendly atmosphere and in spite of profound differences which at times led to heated controversy we and Sir Stafford have parted as friends. The cordiality of the talks was maintained to the last."

(80)

Statement[1] by Maulana Azad[2] **(12th April, 1942)**

Sir Stafford Cripps is reported to have said in the course of an interview at Karachi before leaving India that Congress leaders first went to see Col. L. Johnson,[3] who acted as a mediator in his personal capacity.

This is likely to create an impression that his mediation was sought by us. Facts, however, are otherwise. On or about April 1, a common friend informed Pandit Jawaharlal

Nehru that Col. L. Johnson was anxious to meet him and would be glad if a meeting could be arranged at his residence. Accordingly, Pandit Nehru met him, Again it was by a pure accident that on April 3, while I was on my way to a meeting of the Working Committee, I went to Pandit Nehru's residence which was on my way to pick him up, and there I found Col. Johnson Naturally, we met and had a brief talk. At the end of this talk, Col. Johnson expressed a desire that in the event of the Working Committee coming to an adverse decision, he should be allowed a chance to see if he could be helpful, before the committee's final verdict was formally communicated to Sir Stafford Cripps. His wish was so obviously in the interest of the common object, namely, successful conclusion of Sir Stafford Cripps' mission, that I saw no objection in complying with it. It is hardly necessary to narrate the rest of the story. But I must make it perfectly clear that nobody on behalf of the Congress sought either Col. Johnson's or President Roosvelt's intervention, although in the very nature of things, Col. Johnson's friendly interest was appreciated.

(81)

Statement[1] issued by Abul Kalam Azad at Calcutta on a Resolution passed by the Madras Congress Legislature Party[2]

(25th April, 1942)

It greatly astonished and pained me that a man like Mr. Rajagopalachari, in spite of his being a member of the Congress Working Committee should have adopted such an attitude. I am in communication with him. I would assure you that any personal relationship, howsoever dear to me, cannot deter me for a moment from discharging my duty as a President of the Congress.

I may point out in this connection that in the Congress organisation only the Provincial Congress Committee is the competent body to represent provincial views—not the Congress Legislature Party. Despite this fact the Party itself was not fully represented in the meeting. The information about the meeting indicates that out of 191 Congress members of both the Houses, only 52 attended the meeting. And when votes were taken only 36 participated in the voting. It clearly shows that it would be wrong to attribute the decision to the majority of the Congressmen of the province.

(82)

Statement[1] issued by Abul Kalam Azad on the question whether it was desirable for Provincial and other Congress Committee to function at a time when most of the members of such Committees were out of jail. (25th April, 1942)

Letters have been received from some Provinces asking whether in view of the fact that most of the members of the Provincial and other Congress Committees are out of jail, it is desirable for the Committees to function.

It seems that these Committees have not grasped the real position in this respect. The constitution was never suspended during the last 15 months. The Committees formed after the last election did not cease to function and there is no reason why their normal activities should not continue. The situation in the beginning of the present struggle was that the Congress had asked the members of the Committees to offer Satyagraha. And when all or most of the members were arrested, Gandhiji instructed them not to fill the vacancies thus caused and the offices were put in charge of an organiser during the state of emergency. It did not, however, mean the suspension of the Committees. Now, when all the members of the Committees have come out of the jails, there is no reason why the Committees should not function as before.

(83)

Maulana[1] Azad's Appeal in respect of Medical Unit for Relief of Evacuees[2] (28th April, 1941)

"The Government of India have accepted our offer to organise and send a full medical unit with helpers and volunteers and equipment along the Manipur Road to Sittang in Burma to give help to the evacuees and refugees coming to India. We are, therefore, taking immediate steps to organise such a unit and Dr. Bidhan Chandra Roy, Chairman, Civil Protection Sub-committee, has been requested to organise it in co-operation with the non-official relief organisations. This unit will consist of 8 doctors, 8 compounders, 2 sanitary inspectors, 40 sweepers and personal attendants with medical stores and equipment. The sending of this unit will cost a considerable sum of money but the object is such that I am sure sufficient funds will be forthcoming. The need is immediate. I appeal, therefore, for donations for this medical unit and for relief work among the evacuees coming from Burma. Donations should be sent to the A.I.C.C. Office, Swaraj Bhawan, Allahabad, or to Messrs Bachhraj & Co., Ltd., 5 Mahatma Gandhi Road, Bombay, or to Shri Brij Mohan Birla, Treasurer, Civil Protection Sub-committee of the Bengal Provincial Congress Committee, Birla Park, Ballygunje, Calcutta.

(84)

Maulana[1] Azad's Statement[2] **(7th August, 1943)**

The President, Maulana Abul Kalam Azad, in a statement before putting the Working Committee's resolution to vote, said that the Congress had been trying to bring about unity but every time an effort was made the door was closed from the other side. If the Muslim League was willing to negotiate, he would persuade the Congress within twenty four hours to start negotiations. But every time he had attempted a settlement, the door was closed and barred.

Several attempts had been made by him during the last two years to arrive at a settlement but it always proved to be a one-sided effort. The other side was not willing to come forward to discuss the question. Even during the Allahabad meeting of the A.I.C.C., he made it clear to Rajaji that the Congress was willing to discuss the question and was prepared to start negotiations.

Continuing the Maulana stated that the position of the Congress was well-known. It had always kept the door for negotiations open, What was the use of telling the Congress to arrive at a settlement when it was always prepared to do so and had kept the door for negotiations open ? What was required of those who were shouting for Hindu-Muslim settlement was not to shout at those who kept the door open, but to go and break their heads at the other door which was not only shut but bolted with nails driven so that it might not open at all.

(85)

Maulana[1] Azad's Statement[2] **(8th August, 1942)**

In the present world conflagration, India could side with only one set of combatants. But for India to effectively participate with the right side in this war, it was necessary to properly mobilise the people of India. The present circumstances did not help in enthusing the people to all out effort which would most certainly change the trend of the war. However much one wished, it would not be possible to rouse Indians to enthusiastic participation in this war till the right thing was done by India, namely, the country was made free.

With a view that the position of the Congress and that of India should not be misunderstood the Congress President stated that he had issued a number of statements since the passing of the Wardha Resolution. He was making the United Nations understand that the present move of the Congress was to enable India to take her rightful place in the world conflagration. "Though the resolution had been passed, he was for trying to bring about an understanding till the very last minute. He would try to do everything possible to make the British and the other United Nations understand that a free India would whole-heartedly help the United Nations. He was convinced that such efforts, instead of weakening the Congress case, would strengthen the hands of the Congress. If in spite of such efforts, the United Nations did not respond, the loss would be theirs and not that of India. The Maulana announced that he was sending copies of the resolution to President Roosevelt, to China and to the Russian Ambassador in London. If all their efforts failed, then it was for Indians to take a determined step forward, with the resolve that in this struggle they would venture ahead, no matter what happened to them whether they sank or swam, whether they would win or lose.

(1)

1. Motilal Nehru (1860-1931) entered politics as a Moderate but became an Extremist after the tragedy of Jalianwala Bagh; presided over the Amritsar session of the Congress, 1919; founded the Swaraj Party alongwith C.R. Das, 1923; leader in the Central Legislative Assembly; author of the famous Nehru Report; imprisoned during the Civil Disobedience Movement; released on grounds of ill-health and died soon afterwards on 6 May, 1931.
2. This circular letter marked, 'urgent' was issued from 12, Rippon Street, Calcutta, inviting leading Congressmen including Motilal Nehru, C. Rajgopalachari, C. Vijayaraghavachariar to the special Session of the Congress.
3. NMML, AICC, Papers F. 1/1923.
4. The Special Session of the Congress was held at Delhi on 15th September, 1923.
5. Cocanada or Kakinada Session of the Congress held in 1923 was presided over by Maulana Muhammad Ali.
6. When Maulana Azad was released from Alipore Jail after one year's rigorous imprisonment early in 1923, there was a split in the Congress over the question whether the Council Entry Programme should be pursued through the Legislative Council or not. Consequently on the formation of the Swaraj Party, C.R. Das announced his intention to resign from the presidentship of the Congress. In order to resolve the crisis a Special Session of the Congress was held at Delhi under the Presidentship of Maulana Azad. In his presidential address Maulana Azad said, "Unity is all that we need and it is in order to establish it that we have gathered here to day". In the words of Archarya J.B. Kriplani it was his moderate influence that avoided a cleavage at the time between the Pro-Changers and the No-Changers' (Humayun

Kabir, *op. cit.*, p. 377.

7 In his presidential address at the Delhi session of the Congress, Maulana Azad observed, "India being inhabited by people of different religious presuasions, prejudices, disturbances now and then were quite possible but the remedy lay in not giving them a sectarian colour but to blame the guilty and sympathise with the wronged party". (*The Indian Review* XXIV, September 1923, p. 578). He concluded his address with these words, "I appeal to both communities not to trample so cruely upon the national aspirations and hopes—our determination, our courage, our patriotism are under a very great trial" (*The Indian Annual Register*, 1923, p. 95).

8. M. Asaf Ali (1888-1953), prominent nationalist Muslim; Bar-at-Law; practised at Delhi; Member, Indian Home Rule League; participated in the Khilafat and Non-Cooperation Movements; married Aruna Ganguly, 1928: defended Bhagat Singh; Member; Indian Legislative Assembly, 1934-36; Secretary, Congress Parliamentary Board, 1934; detained in Ahmadnagar Fort, 1942-45; Secretary, Indian National Army Defence Committee, 1946; Member, Interim Government, 1946; First Indian Ambassdor to USA, 1947-48; Governor of Orissa, 1948-52; Ambassdor to Switzerland, 1952-53.

(2)

1. S. Srinivasa Iyengar (1874-1941) one of the foremost lawyers of his times; dominated politics of South India in the early decades of the current century; presided over the Gauhati Session of the Congress, 1926; renounced his title and seat in the Legislative Council in protest against repression; left the Congress in later years due to differences with Mahatma Gandhi; passed away in 1941.

2. This telegram was sent from Calcutta to Iyengar at him Mylapore (Madras) address.
3. NMML, S. Srinivasa Iyengar Papers.

(3)

1. This telegram was sent by Maulana Azad from 3A Store Road, Calcutta, to Motilal Nehru at his camp address Kaisar Bagh, Lucknow.
2. Maulana Azad was one of the signatories to the manifesto advising Muslims to co-operate with the Congress on Nehru Report.
3. NMML, Motilal Nehru Papers.

(4)

1. Jawaharlal Nehru (1889-1964), son of Motilal Nehru; educated at Harrow and Trinity; called to the Bar, 1912; started public life from U.P., soon elevated to the Presidentship of the Congress, 1930; elected Congress President thrice and when India attained independence he was chosen the first Prime Minister which office he held till his death on 27th May, 1964.
2. This telegram was sent from Calcutta.
3. NMML, Jawaharlal Nehru Papers.

(5)

1. This telegram was sent from Calcutta.
2. NMML, Jawaharlal Nahru Papers.

(6)

1. Vijiyaraghavachariar (1852-1944) started practice in law, 1882; emerged as one of the greatest figures in South Indian politics; Member of the Madras Legislative Council, 1913; President, Nagpur session of

the Congress, 1915; presided over the Hindu Mahasabha 1931; died on 19th April, 1944.

This letter was issued from 19-A, Ballygunge, Circular Road, Calcutta.

3. NMML, C. Vijiyaraghavachariar Papers.
4. In the year 1927 Hindu-Muslim unity was in the air, while the Hindu-Muslim riots were on the *terra firma* (Pattabhi Sitaramayya. *The History of the Congress*-I, Allahabad, 1935, p. 535). The communal riots had raised their ugly head in 1927 and the worst affected places were Lahore, Nagpur, Bihar, Bareilly and Multan. The Congress organised a Unity conference on 27th October, 1927 which was presided over by Srinivasa Iyengar who wanted to evolve a formula for Hindu-Muslim Unity Iyer, p. 44).

(7)

1. Issued from Calcutta.
2. Ranjit Pandit (———1944) Sanskrit scholar and patriot; married Vijayalakshmi in 1921; imprisoned during Quit India Movement; released on ground of health in 1943; died on 4 January, 1944.
3. NAI, Rajendra Prasad Papers; Valmiki Chaudhary, *Dr. Rajendra Prasad : Correspondence and Select Documents*, II, New Delhi, 1984, p. 193.

(8)

1. Rajendra Prasad (1884-1963), a brilliant lawyer and prominent Congress leader; President of the Congress, 1939; President of Constituent Assembly; first President of Independent India (1950-62); died 28 February, 1963.
2. Issued from Calcutta.

3. NAI, Rajendra Prasad Papers; Choudhary, *op cit.* II, p. 94.
4. Maulana Azad, with Subhas Bose, Congress President, went to Shillong to resolve the Assam crisis and succeeded in forming a coalition cabinet with five Hindu and three Muslim members. *The Indian Annual Register*, II, 1938, p. 292.

(9)

1. Issued from Calcutta.
2. This perhaps refers to the charges of alleged atrocities on Muslims.
3. ǀAI, Rajendra Prasad Papers; Choodhary, *op. cit*, II, p. 126.

(10)

1. Nilakantha Das was a dissident Congress leader who opposed Biswanath Das, Primer of Orissa: lived in village Sri Ramachandrapur, P.O. Sokhigopal, District Puri.
2. Godavarish Misra, M.L.A. and Joint Editor, *Lakamata* of Orissa; lived at Banpur, District Puri.
3. Chintamani Misra, lieutenant of Nilakantha Das in opposing Biswanath Das.
4. Issued from Calcutta.
5. NAI, Rajendra Prasad Papers; Choudhary, *op. cit.*, II, p. 225.

(11)

1. N. Kanungo seems to have been on the personal staff of Biswanath Das as stated by him in his letter of 22 December, 1938 addressed to Maulana Azad, Choudhary, *op. cit.*, II, p. 224.

2. Biswanath Das was summoned to Calcutta in connection with some allegations against him as also to discuss the Orissa Tenancy Amendment Bill.
3. NAI, Rajendra Prasad Papers; Choudhary, *op. cit.*, II, p. 225.

(12)

1. This letter was sent by Maulana Azad from 19—A, Ballygunge, Circular Road, Calcutta.
2. NMML, Jawaharlal Nehru Papers; Jawaharlal Nehru, *A Bunch of Old Letters* (BOL), *Bombay*, 1958, pp. 371-72.
3. Maulana Azad perhaps fractured his leg at Allahabad. Even on 10 July, 1939 he was unable to use his leg and Dr. B.C. Roy was of the view that he would not be able to walk till the middle of August, 1939 (Please see 13 *supra*).
4. Subhas Chandra Bose (1897-1945) was educated at Cuttack, Calcutta and Cambridge, selected for I.C.S. 1920 but resigned and joined the Non-cooperation Movement, imprisoned 1924-27; elected to the Bengal Legislative Council while under detention, 1926; participated in the Civil Disobedience Movement and imprisioned, 1930-31; President of the Congress, 1938; re-elected 1939 but resigned and founded All India Forward Block, 1939; escaped to Germany, 1941; organised Indian National Army; died in a plane crash in 1945.
5. M.K. Gandhi (1869-1948) commonly called Mahatma Gandhi; called to the Bar, 1890; started political life in South Africa (1893-1915); returning to India in 1915 launched several non-violent movements till India attained independence in 1947; assasinated on 30 January, 1948.
6. It was at Tripuri that in 1939 Subhas Chandra Bose was re-elected Congress President by a narrow margin in the teeth of Mahatma Gandhi's opposi-

tion. It proved to be a pyrrhic victory because he was forced to resign mainly due to disunity within the left. (Sumit Sarkar, *Modern India 1885-1947*), Delhi 1983, p. 374).

7. The reference is obviously to the Resolution moved by Govind Ballabh Pant at the Tripuri Session requesting the President to nominate the Working Committee in accordance with the wishes of Mahatma Gandhi. Sitaramayya, *op. cit* , II, p. 110.
8. Considering the momentous issues that were expected to be raised at the open session, it was somewhat surprising that out of 3319 delegates elected from the various provinces only 2285 were present at the Tripuri Session (*Ibid.*, p. 111.
9. This was perhaps in connection with Shia-Sunni dispute at Lucknow: on 2 June, 1939 Maulana Azad issued an appeal and subsequently proposed to undertake an amicable settlement in the Shia-Sunni dispute at Lucknow. The Shias of Lucknow decided to suspend the Tabarra Agitation on 27 August 1939 as a result of talks with Maulana Azad (Iyer, *op. cit.*, pp. 96-97).
10. Sayyid Sultan Ahmed (1888-1963), a Shia Muslim was a judge of Patna High Court; Vice Chancellor of Patna University, (1923-30); Member of Viceroy's Executive Council, 1937; attended the League of Nations as India's delegate, 1938; nominated to the Permanent Court of International Justice at the Hague but the War intervened; died in 1963.

(13)

1. This letter was issued from 19-A, Ballygunge, Circular Road, Cacutta.
2. NMML, Jawaharlal Nehru Papers; Missing in Nehru BOL *op. cit.*
3. Maulana Azad could not attend the meeting of the AICC held at Bombay on 24-27 June, 1939 Zaidi, *op. cit.*

4. Dr. Bidhan Chandra Roy (1882-1962) eminent physician and prominent national leader; Member, Bengal Legislative Council, 1923; Vice-Chancellor, Calcutta University, 1940-42; Chief Minister, West Bengal, 1948-62, died, 1962.
5. Jawaharlal Nehru was deputed by the Working Committee to go to Ceylon to compose the differences between the Indian imnigrants and the Ceylonese. He reached Colombo by air on 16 July, 1939. This visit established closer social relationship between the peoples of India and Ceylon and brought them nearer to each other. Sitaramyya, *op. cit.*, II, p. 119).
6. Indira was at Suisse at that time. She was to leave that place by the end of July 1939. (S. Gopal, *Selected Works of Jawaharlal Nehru* IX, New Delhi, 1977, p. 634, Nehru, *op. cit.*, BOL, p. 379).

(14)

1. Issued from 19-A, Ballygunge, Circular Road, Calcutta.
2. NAI, Rajendra Prasad Papers; Choudhary, *op. cit.*, III, pp. 154-55.
3. The internal dissensions of the Congress became so acute that Subhas Chandra Bose tendered his resignation and Rajendra Prasad was elected as Congress President on 29 April, 1939 (Zaidi, *op. cit*, XII, p. 164).

(15)

1. This letter was issued from 19-A, Ballygunge, Circular Road, Calcutta.
2. NMML, Jawaharlal Nehru Papers.
3. Maulana Azad could not attend Congress Working Committee meeting at Wardha on 9-12 August, 1939 (Zaidi, *op. cit.*, XII, p. 176).

4. Vallabhbhai Patel (1875-1950), prominent lawyer who gave up his lucrative practice and joined freedom movement in 1916; leader of Bardoli Satyagraha, 1928; President of the Congress, 1935; courted arrest severai times; Home Minister in the Interim Government, 1946 and Deputy Prime Minister in independent India, 1947-50; died 1950.
5. Rajendra Prasad was Congress President at that time (Zaidi, *op. cit.*, XII, p. 176).
6. Jawaharlal Nehru was present by special invitation (*Ibid.*, p. 177).

(16)

1. Issued from Lucknow.
2. NAI, Rajendra Prasad Papers; Choudhary, *op. cit.*, IV (1985) p. 61.
3. Maulana Azad requested the Congress President to call Working Committee in view of the impending threat of World War II.

(17)

1. Issued from Lucknow.
2. NAI, Rajendra Prasad Papers; Choudhary, *op. cit.*, VI, p. 78.
3. The British declared War on Germany on 3rd September, 1939. This was followed by an announcement by the Viceory declaring that India was also at War without consulting the political parties, legislatures of provincial ministries. Reginald Coupland, *The Indian Problem*, Oxford, 1944, p. 212.

(18)

1. Issued from Calcutta.
2. NAI, Rajendra Prasad Papers; Choudhary, *op. cit.*, IV, p. 81.

3. The Congress Working Committee met at Wardha from 8 to 15 September 1939 and expressed its displeasure at the flouting of the Indian opinion by the British Government. It appointed a War Committee consisting of Jawaharlal Nehru (Chairman), Maulana Azad and Vallabhbhai Patel to deal with the question in connection with the situation. Mahatma Gandhi was alone in suggesting unconditional support for the British on a non-violent basis. Sitaramyya *op. cit.*, II, pp. 130-35.

(19)

1. This letter was issued from 19-A, Ballygunge, Circular Road, Calcutta over the letter—form of the All India Congress Parliamentary Sub-committee of which Maulana Azad, Vallabhbhai Patel and Rajendra Prasad were members.
2. NMML, Jawaharlal Nehru Papers; Missing in BOL, *op. cit.*
3. Hindustani Board was appointed with Rajendra Prasad as Chairman and Maulana Azad as one of the members in 1938 to prepare an exhaustive scheme for the development of Hindustani, Iyer, *op. cit.*, p. 87.
4. The reference is obviously to Dr. Bidhan Chandra Roy.
5. Goginath Bardoli (1890-1950) prominent nationalist leader who courted arrest several times; leader of the Congress Party in the Assam Legislative Assembly, 1937: Premier of Assam, 1938; resigned in 1939; returned to power as Premier of Assam in 1946.
6. A.K. Muhammad Fazlul Haq (1873-1962) eminent lawyer and leader of Bengal; President, All India Muslim League 1916-21; Member Central Legislative Assembly, 1935; Premier, Bengal, 1939-43; Interior Minister of Pakistan, 1955; Governor of East Pakistan, 1955; died 1962.

(20)

1. Issued from 19-A, Ballygunge, Circular Road, Calcutta.
2. NAI, Rajendra Prasad Papers; Choudhary, *op. cit.*, IV, p. 159.
3. The Congress Working Committee at its meeting held at Allahabad on 19-23 November, 1939 asked the leader of the Congress Legislative Party of Bengal to transfer the Bengal Assambly Fund to Maulana Azad without any further dclay. Zaidi, *op. cit.*, XII pp. 210-11.

(21)

1. Issued from 19A, Ballygunge, Circular Road, Calcutta.
2. NAI, Rajendra Prasad Papers.
3. Congress Working Committee met at Wardha on 19-21 January, 1940 (Zaidi, *op. cit.*, XII, p. 225).
4. Maulana Azad was anxious to go to Punjab because the people of Punjab had lost all hopes of his ever visiting them owing to numerous postponements of his visit.

(22)

1. Issued from 19-A, Ballygunge, Circular Road, Calcutta.
2. NAI, Rajendra Prasad Papers; Choudhary, *op. cit.*, V (1986), pp. 7-8.

(23)

1. Issued from Calcutta.
2. NAI, Rajendra Prasad Papers; Choudhary. *op. cit.*, V, p.28.
3. Maulana Azad and Mahatma Gandhi went to Patna to attend the Congress Working Committee held on

1st March, 1940. It passed a resolution declaring the determination of the Congress to resort to Civil Disobedience unhesitatingly as soon as the organisation was considered fit enough. Iyer, *op. cit.*, p. ,05.

(24)

1. Sarat Chandra Bose (1889-1950), brother of Subhash Chandra Bose and a prominent Congress leader of Bengal; Member of the Bengal Legislative Council, 1927; Member of Bengal Legislative Assembly, 1937; Member of the Interim Government, 1946; Member, Congress Working Committee, 1946-47.
2. This letter was sent to 1, Woodburn Park, Calcutta.
3. NMML, AICC Papers, p. 5/1940.
4. Consequent upon removal of Subhas Chandra Bose from the post of Bengal Pradesh Congress Committee on 11 August, 1940 the AICC set up an *adhoc* Committee to run the Bengal Congress including Maulana Azad, P.C. Ghosh, B.C. Roy and Kiransonkar Roy as members.
5. In his capacity as President and Leader, Congress Parliamentary Party, Sarat Chandra Bose in his note dated 2nd March, 1940 observed, "I regret very much I can not accept this decision. I was informed at 10,00 A.M. that Maulana Shaheb (Saheb) had arrived. That left me no time to discuss the matter with him. The whip issued by me stands and members are requested to vote according to my whip".

(25)

1. Acharya J.B. Kripalani (1888-1982) eminent national leader; joined Mahatma Gandhi in Champaran Satyagraha, 1917; General Secretary of the Congress, 1934-46; courted arrest several times; Member of the Constituent Assembly, 1946-50; Member of

Lok Sabha, 1952-57, 1963 and 1967; died 19th March, 1982.

2. NMML, AICC Papers, CI 1940.
3. Dr. Pattabhi Sitaramayya (1880-1959), eminent physician and national leader; Member, AICC, 1916; contested Congress Presidential election in 1939 but defeated by Subhas Chandra Bose; he was the official historian of the Congress; passed away on 7 December, 1959.
4. Master Tara Singh (1885-1967) eminent Akali leader actively involved in the Gurdwara Reform Movement; President, Shiromani Gurdwara Prabhandhak Committee; pitted against the Khalsa National Party led by Sir Sunder Singh Majithia; raised demand for Azad Punjab in 1946; demanded Punjabi speaking *Suba* in independent India; supplanted by his own protege, Sant Fateh Singh; died 22 November, 1967.
5. Shiromani Akali Dal was a strong and well-known organisation that helped Master Tara Singh to build his supremacy among the Sikhs from 1930 onwards.
6. The National Week was observed throughout the country to propagate the constructive programme of the Congress emphasising Hindu-Muslim Unity, removal of Untouchability and extensive popularisation of Khadi. Maulana Azad issued a statement on this occasion.

(26)

1. Issued from 19-A, Ballygunge, Circular Road, Calcutta.
2. NMML, Jawaharlal Nehru Papers; Nehru, *op. cit.*, BOL, pp. 424-25.
3. The reference is obviously to the Presidential Address that Maulana Azad delivered at the Ramgarh Session of the Congress on 19-20 March, 1940.

(27)

1. Seth Jamnalal Bajaj (1889-1942), national philanthropist and Honorary Treasurer of the Congress, 1920-42; passed away in 1942.
2. Issued from Howrah.
3. NMML, Jamnalal Bajaj Papers.

(28)

1. This letter was issued from Calcutta on AICC letter form.
2. NMML, Jawaharlal Nehru Papers; Missing in Nehru, BOL *op. cit*.
3. V.K. Krishna Menon (1896-1975) educated at Madras and London; cultivated members of the Labour Party during his long stay in London; represented India at UNO 1946-47; India's High Commissioner in London, 1947.52, Defence Minister in Jawaharlal Nehru's Cabinet; died 1975.
4. The reference is obviously to Acharya J.B. Kripalani who was General Secretary of the Congress at that time.
5. When World War II broke out Krishna Menon sent to Jawaharlal Nehru all kinds of proposals for securing the help of interests friendly to India. He also prepared schemes asking for funds from the Congress. On the recommendation of Jawaharlal Nehru, Maulana Azad, as Congress President, granted £ 100 for Krishna Menon's visit to U.S.A. and placed the matter before the Working Committee at its subsequent meeting. Mahatma Gandhi and Sardar Patel told Maulana Azad that they did not like his action but they would say nothing since he had paid the money in good faith. They pointed out that Indians in London were sharply divided in their judgement about Krishna Menon. Later events, observes Maulana Azad, proved that the

Mahatma and the Sardar were right in their suspicition of Krishna Menon (Maulana Azad, *op. cit.*, p. 199).

6. Maulana Azad was Congress President from 1940 to 1946.
7. Govindha Ballabh Pant (1887-1961) eminent Congres leader; Chief Minister of U.P. and then, Home Minister in Jawaharlal Nehru's Cabinet; died in harness in 1961.

(29)

1. This letter was issued from The Mahal, Nainital.
2. NMML, Jawaharlal Nehru Papers, Nehru, *op. cit.*, BOL, pp.432-33.
3. Jawaharlal Nehru was Chairman of the Planning Committee of the Congress which had been given six months to finish its work. When the Congress Working Committee met at Bombay on 21-27 June, 1939 the term of the Planning Committee was extended to 31 March, 1940. Since the Committee could not finish its task by the scheduled date, Maulana Azad invited Jawaharlal Nehru to Nainital to enable him to complete the work (Zaidi, *op. cit.*, XII, p. 176).
4. Achyut Sitaram Patwardhan (1905-) prominent leader of the Congress Socialist Party; joined Civil Disobedience Movement, 1932 and imprisoned several times; Member, Congress Working Committee, 1936; participated in the Quit India Movement and was underground, 1942-46; retired from politics, 1950.
5. Achyut Patwardhan attended the meeting of the Congress Working Committee held on 16-19 April, 1940 at Wardha as a special invitee (Zaidi, *op. cit.*, XII, p. 421).
6. The Congress Working Committee at its meeting held on 15-19 April, 1940 took stock of the situation

as it had developed in the country since the Ramgarh session and considered it necessary to prepare the Congress organisation for *Satyagraha* which was deemed to be inevitable by the Ramgarh Congress (*Ibid.*, p. 423).

7. Imperial Tobacco Cigarette Company's workers began strike on 15 February and ended with the Governor's intervention on 14 June, 1940. Their main demand was for war allowance owing to increased prices. Gopal, *op. cit.*, X. p. 352).

(30)

1. This letter was sent from The Mahal Nainital to Jawaharlal Nehru at his camp address c/o Dr. Khan Saheb, Ex-Premier, Peshawar.
2. NMML, Jawaharlal Nehru Papers; *op. cit.*, BOL, 433-35.
3. The reference is obviously to Jawaharlal Nehru's letter dated Wardha 10 May, 1940 to Dr. Rajendra Prasad, Choudhary, *op. cit.*, V. pp. 30-32.
4. *Ibid.*, p. 31.
5. In April 1940 Lord Zetland announced that negotiation and not dictation was embodied in the undertaking given by His Majesty's Government to examine constitutional field in consultation with representatives of all parties and interests in India. Mahatma Gandhi responded with a declaration that he would do nothing "to embarass" Great Britain although the Congress could not lend its moral influence to England. In the meanwhile Zetland was replaced by L.S. Amery at the head of India Office while the collapse of France produced in India a new feeling in favour of Britain. Mahatma Gandhi declared "we do not seek our independence out of Britain's ruin" and Jawaharlal proclaimed "England's difficulty is not India's opportunity", *The Indian Year Book*, XXVIII, 1941-42, pp. 887-88.

(31)

1. This letter was issued from 19-A, Ballygunge, Circular Road, Calcutta on AICC letter form.
2. NMML, AICC Papers, File No. G-2/1940.
3. The Congress Working Committee met at Wardha on 17-21 June 1940. The following members were present: Sarojini Naidu, Jawaharlal Nehru, Vallabhbhai Patel, Rajendra Prasad, Rajagopalachari, Bholabhai Desai, Shanker Rao Deo, Profulla Chandra Ghosh, Syed Mahmud, Asaf Ali and J.B. Kripalani. As desired by Maulana Azad, all the four special invitees also attended the meeting. Mahatma Gandhi was present in the afternoon sitting of the Committee. There were conflicting views with regard to the attitude of the Congress to the question of participation in the war efforts. After five days delebrations the Working Committee came to the conclusion that they were unable to go the full length with Mahatma Gandhi. But they did recognise that the Mahatma should be free to pursue his great ideal in his own way and, therefore, absolved him from responsibility for the programme and activity which the Congress had to pursue under the conditions then prevailing in India and the world in regard to external aggression and internal disorder (Zaidi, *op. cit.*, XII, p. 423-27).
4. Acharya Narendra Dev (1889-1956), veteran leader of Congress Socialist Party; Member, Congress Working Committee, 1936; President, All India Kisan Sabha, 1939 and 1942; resigned from the Congress and formed Praja Socialist Party, 1948; Vice-Chancellor Lucknow and Benaras Hindu Universities.
5. Vijay Lakshmi Pandit (1900———), sister of Jawaharlal Nehru and eminent national leader; courted arrest several times; Minister, U.P. 1937-39 and 1945-46; Member, Constituent Assembly, 1946;

India's Ambassador U.S.S.R., 1947-49; India's Ambassador to U.S.A., 1949-52; President, U.N. General Assembly, 1953; Indian High Commissioner, U.K., 1954-61, Governor of Maharashtra, 1962-64.

(32)

1. This letter was issued from 19-A, Ballygunge, Circular Road, Calcutta.
2. NMML, Jawaharlal Nehru Papers; Nehru, *op. cit,*. BOL, p. 436.
3. 18th July is obviously a typing mistake. The reference is to Jawaharlal Nehru's letter of 16th July, 1940, Gopal, *op. cit.*, XI, p. 76.
4. On 11 July, 1940 'Maulana Azad had said that it was wrong to say that the Congress had only shown its readiness to defend India and not participate or help in the War. When we passed the resolution every one of us was quite clear on this point that if India's demands were fulfilled it will be the duty of Indians to participate in the war. The resolution had no other meaning in the mind of even a single individual out of the fifteen members of the Congress Working Committee present, Gopal, *op. cit.*, XI, p. 76.
5. Congress Working Committee meeting at Delhi on 3-7 July, 1940 was of opinion that unless the aforesaid declaration is made and a National Government accordingly formed at the Centre, without delay, all efforts at organizing the material and moral resources of the country for defence cannot in any sense be voluntary or as from a free country and will, therefore, be ineffective. The Working Committee declared that if these measures were adopted it would enable the Congress to throw in its full weight in the efforts for the effective organisation of the defence of the country". (Zaidi, *op. cit.*, XII, p. 429).

6. Congress Working Committee met on 25-27 July, 1940 at Poona where Jawaharlal Nehru met Maulana Azad, *Ibid*; p. 431).
7. The reference is obviously to Generallssimo Chiang Kai Shek's letter wherein he expressed full sympathy with Indian aspirations and gave an expression to his solicitude for Indian welfare (Maulana Azad, *op. cit.*, IWF p. 41).

(33)

1. This letter was issued from 19-A, Ballygune, Circular Road, Calcutta.
2. NMML, Jawaharlal Nehru Papers; missing in Jawaharlal Nehru, *op. cit.*, BOL.
3. Kailash Nath Katju (1887-1968) eminent national leader and lawyer; Minister for Justice, Industries and Development, U.P., 1937-39; Member, Constituent Assembly of India; Governor of Orissa 1947-48; Governor of West Bengal, 1948-51; Minister for Home Affairs, Government of India, 1951; died 17th February, 1968.
4. Syed Mahmud (1889-1971), Contemporary of Jawaharlal Nehru at Cambridge; barristar of Patna High Court; participated in freedom struggle and courted arrest several times; General Secretary, Indian National Congress; Minister in Bihar, 1937-39 and 1946-52; Minister of State for External Affairs, 1954-57; died 1971.

(34)

1. Lord Victor Alexander John Hope Linlithgow (1887-1952) British Civil Servant; Chairman of Royal Commission on Agriculture in India, 1926-28; Chairman of Independent Peers 1933; Chairman of Joint Parliamentary Committee on Indian Constitutional Reforms 1933-34; Viceroy of India 1936-43.

2. NMML, AICC Papers, GI/1940.
3. Issued from Calcutta.

(35)

1. Issued from Calcutta.
2. NMML, AICC Papers, GI/1940.

(36)

1. Issued from Calcutta.
2. NMML, AICC Papers, GI/1940.

(37)

1. Issued from Wardha on AICC letter form.
2. NMML, AICC Papers, GI/1940.

(38)

1. This telegram was sent from Calcutta to Seth Jamnalal Bajaj at his Wardha address.
2. NMML, Jamnalal Bajaj Papers.
3. V.H. Jakatdar was Member of Legislative Assembly from Bhandara, Central Privince, disciplinary action was taken against him in Mishra affairs, ban was lifted when he tendered apology.

(39)

1. Issued from Swaraj Bhawan, Allahabad on AICC letter form.
2. NAI, Rajendra Prasad Papers; Choudhary, *op. cit.*, V, pp. 44-45.
3. In the course of an interview at Lahore on 30th December, 1940 Maulana Azad said: 'If India is invaded tomorrow and there is no alternative to defend my country, I will not hesitate to take arms and fight'. (*The Indian Annual Register*, 1940, II, p. 51).

4. Maulana Azad was to meet Mahatma Gandhi at Wardha but was sentenced by the City Magistrate, Allahabad on 8th January, 1941 to 18 months, imprisonment (Iyer, *op. cit.*, p. 126).

(40)

1. This telegram was issued from Calcutta.
2. NMML, Jawaharlal Nehru Papers; missing in Jawaharlal Nehru, *op. cit.*, BOL.
3. Maulana Azad and Jawahar Lal Nehru attended the Congress Working Committee meeting held on 23-30 December 1941 at Bardoli which was momentous. Frustrated by the political impasse, the Congress Right discussed the posibility of returning to office in November, 1941. Rajagopalachari and Bholabhai Desai wanted the Congress to resume parliamentary activities. At Bardoli Rajagopalachari and the Congress Right proposed to offer the co-operation of free India in the defence of the country on a national basis. The Bardoli meeting also discussed Mahatma Gandhi's letter dated 30 December, 1940 addressed to Maulana Azad. In this letter he referred to the Bombay resolution and observed, "I had interpreted it to mean that the Congress was to refuse participation in the present or all war on the ground principally of non-violence. I found to my astonishment that most members differed from my interpretation and held that the opposition need not be on the ground of non-violence. On re-reading the Bombay resolution I found that the differing members were right and that I had read into it a meaning which its letter could not bear. The discovery of the error makes it impossible for me to lead the Congress in the struggle for resistance to war efforts on grounds in which non-violence was not indispensable. I could not, instance identify myself against Great Britain (Zaidi, *op. cit.*, XII, pp. 448-49). Thus Mahatma

Gandhi insisted that there could be no Congress participation in the war as long as the Congress adhered to the principles of non-violence. There was a split in the Congress on this issue. Maulana Azad publicly stated that "the issue before the Congress is not violence *versus* non-violence but in the British Government's attitude towards the Indian demand. If Britain changes her attitude and makes an offer, the Congress would consider. As far as non-violence is concerned the Congress has made it clear last year in Wardha statement that it could not accept non-violence for the purpose of meeting external aggression. That position still stood." (*The Leader*, 24 December, 1941, p. 9). Thus there was a split in the Congress. Some of the members of the Congress Working Committee threatened to resign. Rajendra Prasad, Sardar Patel and others issued statements urging the AICC members to exercise individual judgement. (Iyer, *op. cit.*, p. 135).

(41)

1. This telegram was sent from Calcutta to Wardha.
2. NMML, Jamnalal Bajaj Papers,
3. Maulana Azad went to Wardha in order to preside over the meeting of the AICC held on 14-16 January, 1942. Starting the proceedings of the AICC, Maulana Azad reviewed the political events during the last 16 months. Alluding to the Bardoli resolution, Maulana Azad said, "We are now exactly where we stood 16 months ago. We have not budged an inch from that position." Referring to the difference of outlook between himself and Mahatma Gandhi, Maulana Azad said, "Mahatma Gandhi had a mission in life, not only for India, but for the whole world. He had declared that he would not have the independence of India secured

under the shadow of war and on condition that the country should support war. That is not the position with me and others and I am prepared to accept the independence of my country at any moment it is available whether it is during war or peace. My whole and only object is the attainment of the freedom of Hindustan. It does not matter if it is attained under the shadow of war. The only thing is that it should be real independence." (*The Leader*, 16 January, 1942, p. 1).

(42)

1. NMML, Jawaharlal Nehru Papers; Missing in Nehru, BOL, *op. cit.*
2. This letter was sent from Calcutta to Anand Bhavan, Allahabad.
3. Addressing a public meeting on 3 February, 1942 at Allahabad, Maulana Azad referred to the co-operation in war and said that first the Congress wanted to bring about conditions which would enable people to live with honour but that door was closed by the British Parliament (*The Leader*, 4 February, 1942, p. 4).

(43)

1. This letter was sent from 19-A, Ballygunge, Circular Road, Calcutta to Anand Bhavan, Allahabad.
2. NMML, Jawaharlal Nehru Papers; Missing in Nehru, BOL, *op. cit.*
3. Since the outbreak of the War, China held that unless India became a voluntary participant in the War she would not render the help of which she was capable. Early in 1942 the Chinese Government was informed by its intelligence service of the statement from Tokyo that the War must be extended to India" (Ram Manohar Lohia, *The Mystery of Sir Stafford*

Misston, Bombay, 1942, p. 9). The peril to India helped to bring nationalism and internationalism close together, the only separating factor being the policy of the British Government (Jawaharlal Nehru, *Discovery of India*, Calcutta, 1946, p. 459). Generalissimo Chiang Kai Sheik arrived in Delhi on 9 February, 1942 in order to discuss the War situation not only with the Viceroy and the Commander-in-Chief but also with the Congress leaders. On 11 February, 1942 at a meeting with Maulana Azad and Jawaharlal Nehru, Chiang Kai Sheik observed that if the British Government offered self-government in the Dominion Status, the Congress should not reject it. Maulana Azad said that, "If during the War the British Government offered Dominion Status and agreed that Indian representatives could work with a sense of freedom and responsibility, the Congress would not refuse the offer" (*The Leader*, 18 February, 1942). Before he left Chiang Kai Sheik made a fervent appeal demanding national government for India but he obviously failed to convince the British Government.

(44)

1. This was issued on AICC letter form from Calcutta.
2. NMML, Jawaharlal Nehru Papers; missing in Jawaharlal Nehru, *op. cit.*, BOL.
3. Miss. Mirdulla Sarabhai (1911-74) eminent Congress leader; Member, Bal Sena, 1920-25 and Youth Movement, 1925-30; General Secretary of the Congress, 1946; imprisoned several times; organised relief and rehabilitation of refugees including abducted women during partition; died 19th October, 1974.
4. Mrs. Aruna Asaf Ali (1909-) married Asaf Ali; worked underground during Quit India Movement; President, Delhi Pradesh Congress Committee,

1947-48; Mayor of Delhi, 1958-60; winner of Lenin Peace Prize; Chair-person of the daily *Patriot*.

5. Mrs. Iftikharud Din, wife of Mian Iftikharud Din (1907-62) who joined the Congress in 1935 and was detained during the Quit India Movement. He joined the Muslim League in 1946 and became Minister for Rehabilitation in Pakistan in 1947.
6. Mrs. Sucheta Kripalani (1903-74), married Acharya Kriplani 1936; Secretary, Women Section of the Congress, 1939; Worked underground, 1942-44; Member, Congress, Working Committee, 1947, General Secretary of the Congress, 1959; Chief minister of U.P. 1963-64.

(45)

1. This circular letter was issued from 19-A, Ballygunge, Circular Road, Calcutta. It was obviously addressed to all the members of the Congress Working Committee.
2. NMML, Jawaharlal Nehru Papers.
3. The reference is obviously to Churchill's announcement of Sir Stafford Cripps Mission on 11 March, 1942. The fall of Rangoon on 21 February and that of Singapore on 8 March, 1942, spurred White Hall to make a show of working for political change in India. Pressure from the U.S.A; the Congress Right and Attlee, the Lord, Privy Seal, induced Churchiil to propound the Great Scheme Anita Inder Singh, *op. cit* , p. 73).

(46)

1. NMML, C. Vijiayaraghavachariar Papers.
2. This was issued on the AICC letter form from 19-A, Ballygunge, Circular Road, Calcutta.
3. The Japanese attack on Pearl Harbour on 7 December, 1941 followed by a succession of lightening

strikes against Shanghai, Hong Kong, the Phillipines, Malaya, Indo-China and Thailand left the Allied forces reeling on every front. On 15 February 1942, Japanese conquest of Singapore followed by attack on Burma in early March 1942 brought the Japanese almost to India's border.

(47)

1. This was issued from Calcutta on the letter form of the AICC.
2. NMML, Jawharlal Nehru Papers; Nehru, *op. cit.*, BOL, pp. 465-66.
3. As a result of the Japanese invasion of Burma in March, 1942 and the rapid occupation of that country, the menace of war was soon at Bengal's door-steps. The panic retreat of the British to India had shown that the colonial apparatus had been ill-prepared for the defence of the country. In view of anticipated Japanese attack, Maulana Azad started organising bands of volunteers. The scheme he had in view was that as soon as Japanese army reached Bengal and the British army withdrew towards Bihar the Congress should step in and capture power in the interregnum before the Japanese could establish themselves (Maulana Azad, *op. cit.*, IWF, p. 74).
4. Khan Abdul Ghaffar Khan popularly known as Badshah Khan (1891-1987), brother of Dr. Khan Saheb and prominent Congress leader of N.W.F. province; courted arrest several times; founded the *Khudai Khidmatgar* or Red shirt organisation, 1929; detained by Pakistan Government for demanding Pakhtoonistan; received the Nehru Award for International Understanding, 1969; received Bharat Ratna-1987; died 1987.
5. The statement was issued on 7 July, 1940 (74 infra) stating that Bholabhai Desai and Asaf Ali had been

deputed to report on the grave situation in Wazirstan. *The Indian Annual Register*, I, 1941, p. 117.

6. Subhas Chandra Bose escaped house arrest on the eve of his trial in 1941 and journeyed in disguise across northern India to Afghanistan. He flew from Kabul to Moscow and from Moscow to Berlin. He was welcomed by Hitler in Germany where he organised Free Indian Legion in Berlin. He was given high powered radio facilities to beam daily broadcasts to India urging his country-men to rise in revolt against British tyranny. From Germany he went to Singapore in the spring of 1943. Sarkar, *op. cit.*, pp. 383, 410-11.

(48)

1. Issued from Wardha
2. NAI, Rajendra Prasad Papers; Choudhary, *op. cit.*, V, p. 143.
3. Though Rajendra Prasad could not attend, Mahatma Gandhi was present at the Congress Working Committee meeting at Wardha on 17-18 March, 1942 (Zaidi, *op. cit.*, XII, p. 461). The urgency of the meeting is obvious as the war had come nearer India. Roosevelt raised the question of Indian political reform in his talks with Churchill in Washington in December, 1941 and in February, 1942 Chiang Kai Sheik during his visit to India had publicly expressed sympathy for India's aspirations for freedom. All this provided an opening for the pro-Indian groups in Britnia and Sir Stafford Cripps, Labour Member of the British War Cabinet, was sent to India early in March 1942 (Sarkar, *op. cit.*, p. 385).

(49)

1. Issued from Sevagram, Wardha.

2. NMML, AICC Papers, GI,/1942.
3. Sir Richard Stafford Cripps (1889-1952) British Statesman, eminent Labour leader and Member of War Cabinet, sent to India twice, first in 1942 and again in 1946 with Cabinet Mission, to effect a peaceful settlement on the Indian political and constitutional problems.

(50)

1. NMML, AICC Papers, GI/1942.
2. B. G. Kher (1888-1957), eminent Congress leader from Maharastra; joined freedom struggle, 1922 and imprisoned several times; Premier of Bombay (1937-39); arrested in 1940; Premier of Bombay again in 1946; died 1957.
3. Ravishankar Shukla (1877-1956), Premier of Central Provinces, 1938-39 and Chief Minister 1956-56; died 1956.
4. Biswanthdas (1889...) a leading Congressman from Orissa; Premier of Orissa, 1937-39; Member, Constituent Assembly, 1947-51, Governor of U.P., 1962-67, Chief Minister, Orissa, 1971-72.
5. Srikrishna Sinha (1887-1961), lawyer of Monghyr, joined Non-Cooperation Movement, 1920; courted arrest several times; Premier of Bihar, 1937-39, Chief Minister of Bihar, 1946-61.

(51)

1. Issued from Birla House, New Delhi.
2. NMML, AICC Papers G26/1942, pt. II.

(52)

1. This was issued from Birla House, New Delhi.
2. NMML, AICC Papers, G26/1942, pt. II.

3. This resolution was passed by the Congress Working Committee at its Delhi session held on 29 March to 11 April, 1942 (Zaidi, *op. cit.*, XII, p. 458).
4. The Draft Declaration, Cripps brought to India, envisaged post-war Dominion Status to India leaving the Dominion free to remain in or to secede from the Common wealth; elections to the provincial legislatures to be held after the war; the Lower House then to act as a single election college and elect the constitution making body by propotional representation; the constitution thus framed to be accepted by Britain subject to the right of any province that was unwilling to accept the new constitution to secede from the Union and in that case the British government would be prepared to agree to a new constitution framed by the seceding provinces, Nicholas Manserghed. *The Transfer of Power* (TP), London 1970, pp. 565-66.
5. Clause (e) of the Declaration invited immediate and effective participation of the leaders of the principal sections of the Indian people in the counsels of their country on urgent issues but insisted that the British during the War would have to retain the control and direction of the defence of India. Maulana Azad and Jawaharlal Nehru, the official negotiators of the Congress' focussed the talks throughout on the provisions for the insured life changes indicated in clause (e). They were apparently told by Cripps that the new Executive would approximate to Cabinet government not formally (as the 1935 Act could not be changed in war time) but in practice through convention, *Ibid*, p. 566.
6. For details see *ibid.*, pp. 683-84.

(53)

1. This was issued from Birla House, New Delhi.
2. NMML, AICC Papers E.G./26/1942.

3. For details *see* Mansergh, *op. cit.* TP, I, pp. 732-33.
4. In respect of defence too there seemed to have been agreement between the Congress negotiators and Cripps in sight on 9 April, 1942. In the presence of Colonel Johnson, President Roosevelt's personal representative, who had come to New Delhi to discuss military problems a compromise formula had been worked out by which an Indian would be in charge of the Defence Department while the British Commander-in-Chief would retain control over field operations and head a War Department whose functions were specified. In the meanwhile the Viceroy Linithgow and Commander-in-Chief Wavel were seriously worried that Cripps was concding too much real power to the Congress and in concert with Premier Churchill they succeeded in blocking the settlement at the last moment. The War Cabinet in its cable of April 1942 sharply pulled up Cripps for not adequately consulting Linithgow and Wavell as also for giving Johnson too much scope. It further deplored allusion to a National Governme t and emphasized the need to bring the whole matter back to Cabinet Plan which he went but to urge (Mansergh, *op. cit*., TP., I, pp. 707-708).

(54)

1. This was issued most probably from Allahabad to Dr. B.C. Roy at his address 36, Wellington Street, Calcutta. The AICC meeting presided over by Maulana Azad was held at Allahabad on 29 April-2 May, 1942 (Zaidi, *op. cit.*, XII, p. 382).
2. NMML, B.C. Roy, Papers G-31, Pt. 2/1942.
3. The Medical Unit was set up by the AICC under Dr. B.C. Roy for the relife of evacuees coming from Burma. *The Indian Annual Register* I January-June, 1942, p. 302.

4. The appeal was issued on 28 April, 1942 (for details please see 83 *supra*).

(55)

1. This was sent over AICC letter form from Calcutta to Achary J.B. Kripalani's office address, Swaraj Bhawan, Allahabad.
2. NMML, AICC, F. 17/1940-42.

(56)

1. This was issued from Calcutta on AICC letter form.
2. NMML, Jawaharlal Nehru Papers; missing in Nehru, *op. cit.* BOL.

(57)

1. This was issued from Calcutta on AICC letter form.
2. NMML, Jawaharlal Nehru Papers; Nehru, *op. cit.*, BOL, pp. 478-79.
3. Rafi Ahmed Kidwai (1894-1954) joined Non-Co-operation Movement 1921; Chier whip of the Swaraj Party, Central Assembly, 1926; Minister, Revenue, Home and Jails in U.P., 1937-39; Minister, Government of India, 1947-54.
4. Sri Krishna Datt Paliwal, a prominent worker of U.P., imprisoned during Salt Satyagraha in 1930; arrested on 6th June, 1942; Minister for Finance and Information in U.P., 1947-48: President, United Forward Republican Block in U.P.; rejoined the Congress, 1963.
5. Rafi Ahmed Kidwai was arrested on 12th May, 1942 under the Defence of India Act.
6. In case of Japanese attack the British Government had decided to follow the scorched earth policy. They had prepared plans to blow up important bridges and to destory factories and industrial instal-

lations. There was great anxiety and unrest in the whole area (Maulana Azad, *op. cit.*, IWF, p. 73).

7. Mian Iftikharud Din, well-known Socialist leader; joined Congress in 1935; detained during the Quit India Movement; joined the Muslim League 1946; Minister for rehabilitation in Pakistan, 1947; expelled from the party 1950; founded Azad Pakistan Party 1951; Founder Member, National Awamy Party.

(58)

1. This was sent on AICC letter form from Calcutta to Acharya J.B. Kripalani at Swaraj Bhawan, Allahabad.
2. NMML, Jawaharlal Nehru Papers.

(59)

1. This was issued on AICC letter form from Culcutta.
2. NMML, Jawaharlal Nehru Papers; missing in Jawaharlal Nehru, *op. cit.*, BOL.
3. Maulana Azad had to cancel his visit to Bombay because during May 1942 he was busy building up public resistance against anticipated Japanese attack, Maulana Azad, *op. cit.*, IWF, p. 74.
4. Failure of negotiations with Sir Stafford Cripps had a profound effect on Rajagopalachari who thought that the independence of India was held up because of the differences between the Congress and the League (*Ibid*, p. 68). His resolution acknowledging the Muslim League's claim to self-determination was defeated by the AICC at its Allahabad meeting held on 29 April-2 May, 1942 (Zaidi, *op. cit.*, XII, p. 390). Mahatma Gandhi chided Rajagopalachari, "He yields the right of secession now to buy unity

in the hope of keeping away the Japanese. I consider the vivisection of India to be a sin" (*Harijan* 24, 31 May and 7 June, 1942). Despite his defeat in the AICC, Rajagopalachari sponsored a resolution in the Madras Congress Legislature Party which was in fact a repudiation of the Congress stand. When Maulana Azad read about the resolution in the newspapers, he was greatly perturbed. He thought thatif one of the members of the Congress Working Committee went about preaching against the decision of the Congress, it would not only weaken the discipline of the organisation but create confusion in the public mind and give a handle to the imperial power (Maulana Azad, *op. cit.*, IWF, pp. 68-69). It was perhaps to resolve this issue that Maulana Azad wanted Jawaharlal Nehru to visit Madras. Rajagopalachari subsequently offered his resignation from the Congress Working Committee.

(60)

1. This letter was issued from Calcutta.
2. NMML, AICC Papers.

(61)

1. This letter was issued on AICC letter form from Calcutta.
2. NMML, AICC Papers.
3. Ram Manohar Lohia (1910-67), eminent Socialist leader; joined the Congress early in life and actively participated in the Quit India Movemeni; joinea the Praja Socialist Party in 1953 but left it in 1956 to form the Socialist Party; Member of Parliament, 1963-67; died on 12 October, 1967.

(62)

1. Issued from Calcutta on AICC letter form.
2. NMML, Jawaharlal Nehru Papers; missing in Nehru, *op. cit.*, BOL.

(63)

1. Issued from Calcutta on AICC letter form.
2. NMML, Jawaharlal Nehru Papers; missing in Nehru, *op. cit.*, BOL.
3. Maulana Azad could not proceed to Wardha as he was busy during May-June, 1942 gearing up the Congress organisation in building up public resistance against the anticipated Japanese attack on Calcutta, (Maulana Azad, *op. cit.*, IWF, p. 74).

PART II

APPEALS AND STATEMENTS

1. Ravindra Kumar and D.N. Panigrahi, eds. *Collected Works of Motilal Nehru*, II, New Delhi, 1984, pp. 283-89.
2. These are English extracts of the long Urdu statement made by Maulana Azad on 11 January, 1922 before the Chief Presidency Magistrate of Calcutta. He was charged with instigating revolt by his two speaches which he delivered at Mirzapur in July, 1921. In these speaches he was reported to have urged Indians in general and Muslims in particular to start a compaign of Non-Cooperation. The Chief Presidency Magistrate, in his judgement on 9 February, 1922 observed, "the Maulana had through his speeches tried to spread a feeling of ill-will and hatred against the established laws of the Government and, therefore, found himself guilty Rajput, *op. cit.*, p. 99). Referring to this trial

trial Maulana Azad later on he wrote, "The trial was agonizing, and yet I tried to rise equal to the occasion. This was a bitterest cup fate ever held to my lips. I drank its contents without the slightest demur." (Humayun Kabir, *op. cit.*, p. 128).

3. The after-math of the World War I brought such wide disillusionment to India that Mahatma Gandhi launched his Non-Co-operation Movement on 1 August, 1920, the day Tilak died.
4. This goes a long way to prove that Maulana Azad was very conscious of the part he was playing in the drama of history. He saw himself cast in the same role as that of Jesus, Socrates, Gallileo—all victimes of unjust courts. In fact from 1910 until his imprisonment in 1921 he throught himself as sort of *Mujaddid* (Rellgious Reformer) at the head of *Hizbullah* (Party of God) which would unite all Indians in liquidating Britist Imperialiam. (Douglas, *op. cit.* p. 97)
5. The Pan-Islamic Khilafat Movement was launched be the Ali Brothers in 1919 championing the cause of Ottoman Khalifa (Caliph) whose empire was proposed to be dismembered by the victorious Allies. Mahatma Gandhi supported the Khilafat Movement and thereby succeeded in winning the support of mass Muslims following for his Non-Co-operation Movement but the Khilafat Movement died In 1924 with Kamal Ataturk's abolltion of the institution of Caliphate unleashing frustrations in India which witnessed worst decade of communal rioting.
6. While launching the Non-Cooperation Movement Mahatma Gandhi had prominssed his followers *Swaraj* in one year by 31 December, 1921 but the entire Movement was abruptly called off on 11 February, 1922 at the insistence of Mahatma Gandhi following the news of the burning alive of 22 policemen by angry peasants at Chauri Chaura, in Gorakhpur district of U.P. (Sarkar, *op. cit.*, p. 206).

7. Maulana Azad thought that his political life began in 1910 soon after his return from Iraq, Egypt, Turkey and France where he came in contact with Arab, Iranian and Turk revolutionaries engaged in anti-imperialist activities. He was more convinced than ever that the Indian Muslims must co-operate with their compatriots in the work of political liberation of their country (M.Azad, *op.cit.*, IWF, p.7). In order to propagate his ideas he wrote an article entitled '*Nandwatul Ulama and the Goal of Indian Muslims.* In this article, published in April, 1910, he says that the modern education of the Aligarh variety had produced only job hunters and that the only hope for Indian Muslims lay in following the lead given by Maulana Shibli at Nadwa. (S.M. Ikram, *Modern Muslim India and the Birth of Pakistan*, Lahore, 1965, p. 126.
8. He was 18 years old in 1906. It was in this year that he got a glimpse of the effectiveness of political activism in Calcutta which was then in the throes of the Swadeshi Movement. He was very much impressed by the activities of Hindu revolutionaries whose mistrust, however, did not allow any Muslim to join their secret societies. Maulana Azad claims to have convinced them that it was wrong to condemn the entire Muslim community as anti-Hindu and argued that active hostility or even the indifference of Muslims would make the struggle for political liberty much more difficult. He thus gained their confidence and was allowed to join one of their secret societies through the mediation of Shyam Sunder Chakravarty, an associate of Sri Aurobindo Ghose. Maulana Azad, *op. cit.*, IWF, pp. 4-6.
9. He was interned at Ranchi from 20 May, 1916 to 25 December 1919. During this period he was engaged in writing his *Tazkira* which though intended to be an autobiography turned out to be annals of the heroes of the Islamic history.

10. *Al-Hilal*, an Urdu Weekly, was launched by Maulana Azad from Calcutta on 13 July, 1912 with the twin objects of challenging the traditional interpretation of Islam and turning his co-religionists from British loyalism to composite nationalism and anti-colonialism. "He", according to Acharya Kripalani, "viewed the question of India's freedom in the context of colonialism in general and the Islamic lands in particular. For him, the emancipation of India from the shackles of British imperialim was a necessary condition for breaking the chains that had been and were being forged by western imperialist nations, principally British, to bind Islamic lands, For Maulana, therefore, the Indian national struggle was not only a duty to the motherland but to Islam" (J.B. Kripalani in Humayun Kabir, *op. cit.*, Memorial p. 301). *Al-Hilal* soon invited the wrath of British Government which confiscated *Al-Hilal* press on 18 December. 1914. Maulana Azad started *al-Balagh* on 12 November, 1915 but it also met the fate of *al-Hilal* on 31 March, 1916 (Douglas, *op. cit.*, p. 98). According to V. Vivian, Assistant Director, Criminal Intelligence Department, Maulana Azad and Obedullah Sindhi secretly met at Delhi in January, 1915, worked out details of their plot and despatched a party of students to Kabul" (NAI Home Political, A, June, 1919 No. 590 Appendix I). He was also responsible for sending a bomb-maker and a Bengali doctor to Kabul (NAI, Home Political, A, June, 1919 No. 519 Appendix I). It was at the instance of Maulana Azad that Maulana Mahmudul Hasan, Principal of Deoband College, set out on his mission to Hijaz on 18th September, 1915" (NAI, Foreign and Political, Frontier Branch, Confidential-A, 1918 Nos. 214-434, Appendix I). In his note dated 7 April, 1916, W. Sealy of the Bihar Criminal Intelligence Department observes, "Maulana Azad is an extremist agitator" (Home Political, May, 1916, No. 455 Enclosure). Thus Maulana Azad

was involved in violent revolutionary activities to liberate his country from the British bondage. He himself could not go to Kabul to join the first provisional Government of India on foreign soil as he was interned at Ranchi on 20 May, 1916 under the Defence of India Act (Home Political A, May, 1916 No. 456).

(65)

1. *The Bombay Chronicle*, 4 May, 1923.
2. Failure of Mahatma Gandhi's promise in 1920 of Swaraj within a year combined with abrupt calling off of Non-Cooperation Movement on 11 Februery, 1922 because of Chauri Chaura incident resulted in a sense of anti-climax and disillusionment. At the same time, the British Colonialists started to fan hostilities between Hindus and Muslims through communal organisations. The Hindu-Muslim unity of 1919-22 was quickly followed by communal riots on an unprecedented scale (Sarkar, *op. cit.*, p. 226).
3. The Moplah uprising was triggered off by a Police raid on Tirurangadi mosque in search of arms on 20th August 1921, with widespread attacks on police stations. public offices and houses of oppressive Nambudri landowners. Gradually this uprising spread over a considerable part of Malabar and developed into a struggle of the Muslim Moplah tenants against the Hindu Nambudri land-owners. Despite the religious aspects of this struggle the Moplah uprising was both anti-fedual and anti-colonial in nature (G. Kotovsky, *India in Modern ,Times*, II, Moscow, 1979, p. 169.
4. The Hindu Maha Sabha at its 1923 session made appeals for the forcible conversion of Indian Muslims to Hinduism. It, thus, joined hands with *Arya Samaj* in its compaign of *Shuddhi* (purification) and reconversion of Muslims initially in Punjab by forcing Muslims to wash away their pollution with

total immersion in a river or water-tank. *Shuddhi* and *Sanghatan* (Organisation) provoked *Tabligh* (Propagation) and *Tanzim* (Organisation) among Muslims. The growth of communal associations led to communal rioting and the precarious Hindu Muslim unity was further eroded (Sarkar, *op. cit.*, p. 235).

5. Sarojini Naidu (1979-1949) poetess and eminent Congress leader; Fellow, Royal Society of Literature, 1914; connected with Women's movement in India and Welfare of students; First Indian Woman President of the Congress, 1925; delegate Round Table Conference, 1931, Governor, U.P. 1947-49; died 1949.
6. Hakim Ajmal Khan (1865-1927), leading Unani Physician of Delhi and Nationalist Muslim leader; Chairman, Reception Committee, Delhi Session of the Congress, 1918; President Indian National Congress; 1921; died 1927.
7. Swami Shraddhanand (1855-1926), prominent Arya Samajist; participated in politics and joined the Congress; leader of *Shuddhi* Movement resented by Indian Muslims; shot dead in Delhi, 1926.
8. Deshbandhu Chittranjan Das (1870-1925), leading barrister; joined Congress 1906; formed with Motilal Nehru, the Swaraj Party, 1922; President of the Congress, 1922; he was known as Deshbandhu or Friend of the country.

(66)

1. NMML, AICC Papers (Suppl.).
2. Communal riots broke out at Nagpur early in 1924 on the issue of playing of professional music in front of mosques.
3. The Unity Conference was held on 26 September, 1924 at Delhi under the Presidentship of Motilal Nehru. It passed a resolution which declared "that all the points in dispute shall be decided by reference

either to private arbitration or, where that is impossible, by reference to a Court of Law" (Iyer, *op. cit*; p. 37).

(67)

1. The *Indian Annual Register*, II July-December 1926, pp 90-93.
2. Since the Kohat riots of September 1924, the entire country was blazing with the fire of communal frenzy and the principal places affected were Calcutta, Delhi and Allahabad. Maulana Azad and Motilal Nehru wanted to put an end to the long drawn out riots and with this end in view they issued the present manifesto. (Iyer, *op. cit*; p. 41.)
3. The Indian National Union was proposed to be set-up with the object of avoiding conflicts and to bring about a thorough understanding between different communities on a solid and permanent basis. A preliminary meeting of those who expressed their willingness to join the proposed Union was held at Delhi on 10 September, 1926. A sub-committee consisting of Maulana Azad, Sarojini Naidu, K. Santhanam and others was appointed to draft the rules and regulations of the Union and to circulate its report for criticism (*Ibid.*, pp. 42-43).

(68)

1. *The Indian Annual Register, I, 1930, p. 17.*
2. The Congress Working Committee met at Lahore under the Presidentship of Jawaharlal Nehru on 2nd January 1930 and resolved to implement Congress resolution of *Purnaa Swaraj* or complete independence and to observe 26 January as *Purnaa Swaraj Day* all over India. It was on this very day that the present appeal was issued by Maulana Azad and Dr. Ansari as authorised by the Nationalist Muslim Party.

(69)

1. NMML, AICC Papers, F. No. 34/1931.
2. By the Gandhi-Irwin Pact signed on 5 March 1931 the British Government agreed to put an end to repressive measures and to free political prisoners. Mahatma Gandhi publicly halted the civil disobedience campaign and agreed to take part in the Second Round Table Conference. Subhash Bose and other leaders of India's youth read the pact as nothing but capitulation to Government. The frustration and anger of radical nationalists was sharpened by the execution of Bhagat Singh, Sukhdev and Raj Guru on 23 March 1931 just before the opening of the Karachi Congress on 26 March 1931, which approved Mahatma Gandhi's stand. (Sarkar, *op. cit*; p. 311). While the Karachi session was going on, serious Hindu-Muslim riots broke out in a number of cities including Kanpur.
3. Ganesh Shankar Vidyarthi (-1931) Editor, and S. Narayan Mishra, publisher of the Hindi daily *Pratap*, were accused of defamation; on 24 and 25 June 1921 Jawaharlal Nehru appeared as a defence witness in this case; later on Vidyarthi died while trying to prevent Hindu-Muslim riots in 1931 in Kanpur.

(70)

1. *The Indian Annual Register*, II (1939) p. 394.
2. When British entered the World War II in Europe, Lord Linlithgow, Viceroy of India, declared India a belligerent on 3rd September, 1939, without consultation with the representatives of the Indian political parties. This naturally aroused widespread public protest. It was in this context that Maulana Azad and Jawaharlal Nehru issued the present statement.

(71)

1. *The Indian Annual Register II* July-December 1939, pp. 415-16.
2. Soon after the resignation of the Congress ministries in October 1939, Maulana Azad and Jawaharlal Nehru met Mahatma Gandhi and Rajendra Prasad at Delhi and there was an indication of a possible agreement between the Congress and the Muslim League for the settlement of India's immediate political difficulties. Subsequently a proposal to that effect was submitted to the Viceroy early in Nov. 1939 by Rajendra Prasad on behalf of the Congress and by Jinnah on behalf of the Muslim League (Iyer, *op. cit.*, p. 102). It was in this political context that Maulana Azad issued the present statement.
3. Mohamed Ali Jinnah (1876-1948) eminent Barrister of Bombay High Court; President, All India Muslim League, 1916, 1920, 1934 till his death; for many years an ardent nationalist in the early decades of the 20th century but later became champion of Muslim separatism and successfully demanded creation of Pakistan; first Governor General of Pakistan 1947-48; died 1948.

(72)

1. *The Indian Annual Register, I,* January-June 1940, p. 63.
2. Lord Zetland, Secretary of State, made an announcement in ihe House of Lords in April 1940, to the effect that His Majesty's Government wanted to examine constitutional field in consultation with representatives of all parties and interests in India (*The Indian Year Book,* XXVIII, 1941-42, pp. 887-88). It was in this context that Maulana Azad made the present statement.

(73)

1. *The Indian Annual Register I*, January-June, 1940, pp. 242-43.
2. Free from attacking Congress Ministries, Jinnah now focussed his attention on formulating his party's constitutional goal. On 23 March 1940 that goal emerged from the Lahore session of the Muslim League as Pakistan. 'The Problem in India' he observed, 'is not of an inter communal character but, manifestly of an international one and must be treated as such. By international he meant literally as between nations (Anita Inder Singh *op. cit.*, p. 57). Mahatma Gandhi was deeply hurt by the Lahore Resolution denouncing it as a call for the vivesection of India. In order to bolster its single nation theory, the Congress decided to observe the National Week throughout the country with more than usual enthusiasm this year.

(74)

1. *The Indian Annual Register II*, July-December, 1940 p. 177.
2. At the Congress Working Committee meeting held at Delhi on 3-7 July, 1940 Khan Abdul Ghaffar Khan reported that the Government had refused permission to the deputation of the provincial Congress Committee to visit Waziristan to examine the economic conditions of the tribesmen and to render them such aid for their social welfare as was possible. The Congress Working Committee, therefore, decided to appoint Bholabhai Desai and Asaf Ali to proceed to Waziristan and carry on the work that the said deputation would have done and to report to the Working Committee the result thereof (Zaidi *op. cit.*, XII pp. 429-31). It was in this context that Maulana Azad issued the present statement.

3. Bholabhai Desai (1877-1946) leading lawyer and outstanding Congress leader; joined Civil Disobedience Movement and imprisoned 1932; arrested again in 1940; leader of opposition in the Central Assembly for nine years; Member, Congress Working Committee: entered into private negotiations with Liaqat Ali Khan to bring about compromise between Congress and League and paved the way for Simla Conference ; defended Indian National Army prisoners; died in May 1946.

(75)

1. *The Indian Annual Register II,* July-December 1940, pp. 193-94.
2. All India Congress Committee at its meeting held at Poona on 27-28 July, 1940 Maulana Azad made this statement explaining the circumstances leading upto the AICC meeting at Poona to take a final decision on Mahatma Gandhi's stand (in respect of resisting war effort non-violently (Zaidi, *op. cit.*, XII, pp. 373, 549).

(76)

1. *The Indian Annual Register II,* July-Decemoer 1940 pp. 201-02.
2. Japanese southward expansion had begun with the fall of France in June, 1940 when Japanese demands obliged the French to close the Haiphong-Kunming rail-road as a supply route to free China. On 16th July, 1940 the British Government announced its decision to close the Burma-China Road for three months. In fact France was bullied by Japan into closing the door from Indo-China to China and than it tried to repeat these tactics in regard to the Burma China route. It was in this context that Maulana Azad issued the present statement.

(77)

1. *The Indian Annual Register II*, July-December 1940, p. 31
2. All India Congress Committee at its meeting held at Bombay on 15-16, 1940 passed a resolution authorising Mahatma Gandhi to launch *Satyagraha*, if he decided it was a necessary next step, (Zaidi, *op. cit.*, XII, pp. 374-75). On 18th September, 1940. Mahatma Gandhi wrote to the Viceroy seeking an interview and met him on 27 and 30 September 1940 The talks failed (*Ibid.*, pp. 553-54) It was in this context that Maulana Azad made the present statement.

(78)

1. *The Indian Annual Register I*, January-June 1942, p. 332
2. The Jamiatul Ulama held its thirteenth session on 20-22 March 1942 at L ahore. Maulana Azad udressed the concluding session and advising Muslims to work for the independence of the country made the present statement.

(79)

1. *The Indian Annual Register I*, January-June 1942 pp. 236-38
2. The Cripp's Mission was plagued throughout; and ultimately torpedoed by numerous ambiguities and misunderstandings. Churchill had assured Linlithgow that Cripps was bound by the Draft Declaration which was His Majesty's Government's utmost limit but driven by a desire for a settlemnt Cripps seems to have gone considerably beyoned that in his talks with Maulana Azad and Jawaharlal Nehru who were apparently told by Cripps that the new Executive would approximate to cabinet government, not for-

mally but in practice through convention. In his cable to Churchill on 4 April 1942 Cripps referred to the new arrangement whereby the Executive Council will approximate to a cabinet (Mansergh, *op cit.*, TP, p. 636). Similarly by 9 April, 1942 a compromise formula had been worked out in respect of defence. But Cripps Mission was destined to fail because Linlithgow, Wavell and Churchill undercut Cripps by their unwillingeness to grant Indian desire for real, as opposed to potential, authority. (R.J. Moore, *Churchill, Cripps and India, 1930-1945*, London, 1979, pp. 141-44). It was against this political background that Maulana Azad met the Press and told them about his talks with Cripps.

3. Archibald Percival wavell (1883-1950), Commander-in-Chief for the Middle East, 1939-41; Commander-in Chief for India, 1941-42; Viceroy of India, 1943-47 died 1950.

(80)

1. Col. Louis Johnson, a personal representative of President Franklin D. Roosevelt, had come to New Delhi early in April, 1942 to discuss military problems. He was thus, incidentally present when Cripps was conducting negotiations with Maulana Azad and Jawaharlal Nehru (Sarkar. *op. cit.*, p. 387). Jawaharlal Nehru in a statement to the press clarified that Col. Johnson did not interfere in any way, though, of course, he expressed his desire that a satisfactory settlement should be reached. He thanked Col. Johnson for his friendly approach to India's problems though in the nature of things he could not interfere in what was taking place. (*The Indian Annual Register I*, January-June, 1942, p. 242).

2. *The Indian Annual Register I*, January-June 1942, PP. 241-42

(81)

1. The Congress Working Committee at its meeting at Allahabad on 27 April—1 May 1942 as also the AICC at its meetting at Allahabad on 29 April-2 May, 1943 approved the rejection of the Cripps proposals (Zaidi, *op. cit.*, XII, pp. 382, 464) and rejected C. Rajagopalachari's resolution acknowledging Muslima Leagues claim to self-determination. In fact he had been deeply disturbed by the deteriorating communal situation in the country and was of the view that the independence of India was held up because of differences between the Congress and the League. The Cripps Plan, therefore, had profound effect on Rajagopalachari, (Maulana Azad, *op. cit.*, IWF. p. 68). In his capacity as leader of the Congress party in the Madras Assembly Rajagopalachari got two resolutions passed at a specialmeeting of the Congress Members of the Assembly, one urging the resumption of ministerial responsiblities in provinces and the other urging settlement with the Muslim League on the basis of the latter's demand for separation. Both these resolutions were at variance with the declared policies of the Congress (Zaidi, *op. cit.*, XII p. 584). It was in this context that Maulana Azad issued the present statement.
2. NAI, Rajendra Prasad Papers; Choudhary*op. cit.*, V p. 330

(82)

1. NAI, Rajendra Prasad Papers; Choudary, *op. cit.*, V p. 331.

(83)

1. AICC at its meeting held at Allahabad on 29 April -2 May, 1942 noted with indignation the arrangements made for and the treatment accorded to evacuees and refugees from Malaya and Burma to

India. Such arrangements for evacuation as were made were meant principally for the European population and at every step racial discrimination, was in evidence. (Zaidi, *op. cit.*, XII pp. 384-85). It was in this context that Maulana Azad issued the present appeal for funds.

2. *The Indian Annual Register I*, January-June, 1942, p. 309.

(84)

1. The All India Congress Committee met on 7-9 August, 1942 in a spacious and beautifully decorated pandal on the Gowalia Tank Maidan, Bombay. Before putting the Working Committees resolution to vote Maulana Azad referred to several attempts made for Congress-League understanding and made the present statement.
2. *The Indian Annual Register II*, July-December 1942, p. 254

(85)

1. This statement was made by Maulana Azad after the All India Congress Committee adopted the Quit India Resolution.
2. *The Indian Annual Register II*, July December 1942 p. 254.

Bibliography

Primary Sources

A. Public Records

Foreign and Political, Frontier Branch (Confidential) 1918, NAI.
Home Political 1916, 1919, NAI.
Reforms Office, NAI.

B. Private Archives

AICC Papers, NMML.
Jawaharlal Nehru Papers, NMML.
Linlithgow Papers, N.A.I.
Jamnalal Bajaj Papers, NMML.
Motilal Nehru Papers, NMML.
Rajendra Prasad Papers, NAI.
S. Srinivasa Iyengar Papers, NMML.
C. Vijiaraghavachariar Papers, NMML.

C. Documents

Choudhary, Valmiki (ed.), *Rajendra Prasad: Correspondence and Select Documents* II, New Delhi (1984) IV (1985), V (1986).
Gopal, S. (ed.), *Selected Works of Jawaharlal Nehru* IX, XI, New Delhi, 1971-1977.
Malik Ram, (ed.), *Khutbat-i-Azad*, Delhi, 1974.

Mansergh, Nicholas (ed.), *The Transfer of Power* I, London, 1970.

Mehr, Ghulam Rasul (ed.), *Tabarrukat-i-Azad*, Hyderabad, 1959.

Nehru, Jawaharlal, *A Bunch of Letters*, Bombay, 1958.

Pirzada, S.S., *Foundation of Pakistan: All India Muslim League Documents* Vol. III (1924-47), Karachi, 1970.

Zaidi, A M., (ed.), *The Encyclopaedia of the Indian National Congress* XII, New Delhi, 1981.

Secondary Sources

Azad, Maulana Abul Kalam, *India Wins Freedom*, Bombay, 1959, Madras, 1988.

Brecher, Michael, *Jawaharlal Nehru—A Political Biography*, London, 1959.

Coupland, Reginald, *The Indian Problem*, Oxford, 1944.

Douglas, Ian Henderson, *Abul Kalam Azad: An Intellectual and Religious Biography*, Delhi, 1988.

Humayun Kabir, *Maulana Azad: Memorial Volume*, Bombay, 1959.

Iyer, R. Subramania, *Role of Maulana Abul Kalam Azad in Indian Politics*, Hyderabad, 1968.

Ikram, S.M., *Modern Muslim India and the Birth of Pakistan*, Lahore, 1965.

Khaliquzzaman, *Pathway to Pakistan*, Lahore, 1961.

Kotovsky, S., *India in Modern Times* II, Moscow, 1979.

Lohia, Ram Manohar, *The Mystry of Sir Stafford Cripps Mission*, Bombay, 1943.

Masihul Hasan, Sayyid, (ed.), *Hawashi-i-Abul Kalam Azad*, Delhi, 1988.

Mukerji, Hiren, Recelling, *India's Struggle for Freedom*. Delhi 1983.

Moin Shakir, *Azad, Islam and Nationalism*, New Delhi, n.d.

Munshi, K.M., *Pilgrimage to Freedom* (1902-50), Bombay, 1947.

Malihabadi, Abdur Razzag, *Azad ki Kahani, Khud Azad ki Zabani*, Calcutta, 1959.

Mushirul Haq, Azad, *Abul Kalam*, Art in *Dictionary of National Biography*, (ed.), S.P. Sen, Calcutta, 1979.

Rajput, A.B., *Maulana Abul Kalam Azad*, Lahore, 1946.

Shiva Rao, *Framing of India's Constitution—A Study*, Nasik, 1968.

Singh, Anita Inder, *The Origins of the Partition of India, 1936-47*, OUP, 1987.

Sitaramayya, Pattabhi, *The History of the Congress*, Allahabad, 1935.

Servai, H.M., *Partition of India: Legend and Reality*, Bomb 1989.

Periodicals

The Bombay Chronicle, 1923.

Harijan, 1940.

Al-Hilal, 3(22).

The India Quarterly Register I-V.

The Indian Annual Register I-V.

The Indian Year Book XXVII, XXVIII.

The Leader, 1937, 1941, 1942.

National Heralad, 1939-40.

Index